CREATIVITY
&
CONSTRAINT

WISING UP ANTHOLOGIES

ILLNESS & GRACE, TERROR & TRANSFORMATION
2007

FAMILIES: THE FRONTLINE OF PLURALISM
2008

LOVE AFTER 70
2008

DOUBLE LIVES, REINVENTION & THOSE WE LEAVE BEHIND
2009

VIEW FROM THE BED: VIEW FROM THE BEDSIDE
2010

SHIFTING BALANCE SHEETS:
Women's Stories of Naturalized Citizenship & Cultural Attachment
2011

COMPLEX ALLEGIANCES:
Constellations of Immigration, Citizenship, & Belonging
2012

DARING TO REPAIR:
What Is It, Who Does It & Why?
2012

CONNECTED:
What Remains as We All Change
2013

CREATIVITY
&
CONSTRAINT

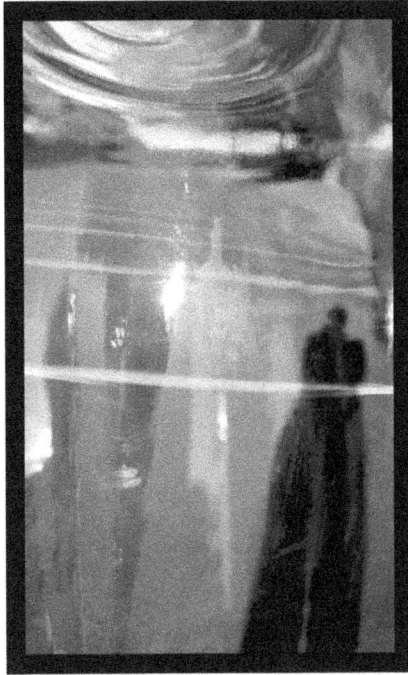

Heather Tosteson, Charles D. Brockett,
Kerry Langan, Michele Markarian
Editors

Wising Up Press
Decatur, Georgia

Wising Up Press
P.O. Box 2122
Decatur, GA 30031-2122
www.universaltable.org

Catalogue-in-Publication data is on file with the Library of Congress.
LCCN: 2014951085

Wising Up ISBN-13: 978-0-9826933-3-9

TABLE OF CONTENTS

IV. Artists' Lives

V. Life . . . Art . . . Life . . .

HEATHER TOSTESON

CREATIVITY & CONSTRAINT

Sharing the idea for an anthology is like lighting a fire under one of those brilliantly colored paper balloons made in Guatemalan pueblos, or corking up a message into an old, salt-scoured bottle and tossing it beyond the surf. It requires a trust in lilt and drift. The act is both a completion and an invitation. We have valued a question that arises out of some incongruence, some essential tension, in our lived life enough to bring it into haphazard relation to other lives, other realities. By voicing the question, setting it aloft or adrift, we are creating "room to reconsider our reality," what Ai Weiwei describes as one of the core purposes of art.

What returns in response often asks something completely different of us. Sometimes it makes us realize we were really asking another question entirely, and now we need to answer both the question we let soar and the one that has returned to us.

There is something resistant, grounding, often miring in this engagement with the other—whether the demands of intellectual order, limits of material properties, intractability of social facts, the scantiness of our own intellect, skill, or temperament. But isn't this what we asked for: real life pushing back? "To a large extent my work is dependent on reality. I don't rely on it for self-expression, but I must connect to it to feel the desire to create," Ai Weiwei observes of his own process. For this resistance also inspires. It is proof that a conversation is taking place.

Anne Truitt, the sculptor, observed in *Daybook*, her first journal exploring her artistic process that if art were only having an interesting idea, we would all be conceptual artists. Instead art is the result of that idea tangling, most intimately, with matter.

> *The ideas in my head are invariably more radiant than what is under my hand. But something puritanical and tough in me won't take that fence. The poem has to be written, the painting painted, the sculpture wrought. . . . Life just seems to me irremediably about coping with the physical.*

Here are some of the questions that we set aloft and adrift almost a year ago:

Material Constraint: We often think of true creativity as unfettered liberty—but is creativity something that only takes root, flourishes, within bounds? William Carlos Williams said, "no ideas but in things." What happens to our ideas if they must stay attached to and work their way through the material world—often being materially changed in the process?

Artistic Transmutation: Why is it that we often feel more empowered, more intimately related within the artifice of a story, a song, a painting than we do in the world at large? What do we learn when we try to take that expansiveness back out into the binding but unbounded world around us? Or take our real world constraints into story?

Social Constraint: What, if anything, do experiences of creativity and constraint have to do with real world challenges, where our desires and drives are checked daily, where our playing fields are far from level, where hard work isn't always rewarded, where dreams can be gaping doorways to despair but where the absence of them can be far worse?

As is not unusual, we read the submissions we received in a rather different place from when we released the call. At about the same time we put out this call, we started on an increasingly ambitious and absorbing non-fiction writing project that explores the lasting consequences of felony convictions in our society. It involves interviewing people throughout the criminal justice system, especially people who have been incarcerated who, even after serving their sentences, struggle with social and legal constraints that would daunt any of us aspiring to full, productive, socially integrated lives. The stories, poems, and memoirs here sometimes feel like they come from a completely different order of existence from the stories we are now invited into daily. But are they really?

I begin this collection by sharing three evocative real life vignettes that come to me as partial responses to those three question sets.

I Have to Be A Sponge

I keep hearing the voice of one man I heard talking in a support group for people impacted by incarceration, a group comprised of people who have worked for years in corrections as counselors or chaplains as well as people who have served prison sentences, some for very long periods. He is a tall, shambling man, driven by anxiety and disorientation to speak urgently, compulsively, his words tumbling over each other. That evening his words eddied around one person and another as he described troubled interactions in one homeless shelter, a transfer to another. "I can't get angry. I have to humble myself. I understand that now. I have to be a sponge. I don't understand nothing out here no more. I have to be a sponge."

He has been released from prison after serving forty-three years. He recognizes nothing in the city of his youth, and, now, of his vertiginous old age. The houses he knew have disappeared. The customs as well. Young men no longer stand up for women or the disabled. "I can't get angry. I have to humble myself. I know nothing no more about this world out here. I have to be a sponge."

"A sponge," he kept repeating. It was, you understand, a mantra filled with hope. If he releases the concepts, even the memories that for forty-three years have been his lifeline to a world beyond the prison, something new, intrinsically ordered and ordering might come to take their place. No idea but in these men in the support group, patiently listening, bearing witness by their very presence to an inconceivable possibility open to him too if only he can bear to be as absorbent, as faithful as a sponge. How many of us, at sixty-six, have that kind of courage?

Break Every Chain

"It was a natural, given my degree in music. As long as I've worked in prisons, I have led a choir," the chaplain told me. She has spent almost thirty years in the state prison system and still loves the work she does. Her experience of her role is as intimately tied up with her understanding of art as it is of religion. The choir performances are the only times these women spend outside prison walls. They are never allowed to know where they are going when they leave to perform. They are always accompanied by armed guards. To be part of the choir, they must have good voices and also have no recent record of disciplinary problems.

The expanded horizon that membership in the choir provides is often a powerful incentive for change. The chaplain described one woman with a beautiful voice who was thwarted by her own impulsivity for over two years before she was able to join the choir. It took her a year to get the mandatory six-month period of good behavior that would allow her to try out. She was selected, but within a week she was again put on disciplinary restraint. She finally came to the chaplain and told her to give the slot to someone else. But the chaplain said, "It is your place. You earned it with your voice. Now you have to earn it with your behavior. It will be there when you do." Within six months she was singing, and traveling, with the choir.

The reward of the choir is not just periodically being released, under close guard, to sing in churches around the state, it is also the release into the experience of singing itself. "I like to help the women get in touch with a time in their lives when they were happier. When they are singing, there is no room for anxiety," the chaplain said. "It is a completely absorbing experience. Transcendent."

For the audience too, we found when one Sunday we visited a modest church in a struggling area of Atlanta to hear the prison choir perform. When we entered, the church members immediately waved us on down the corridor, where we found ourselves among prison staff and choir members busy donning their robes. We turned and went back and explained we were visitors and were led into the sanctuary where an organizational meeting seamlessly morphed into a religious service.

No sooner had we slipped into a pew in the back than we were drawn into the most amazing experience of choral sound. In this unpretentious church, many parishioners in their Sunday school t-shirts, voices rose and fell in effortless harmony led first by a line of deacons, then by a choir in street clothes assembled equally casually in the choir loft. Voices melded, harmonized from above us and on either side in a way that made us feel perfectly held. A woman with an amazing voice sang from the choir stall then returned to the pew behind us to hold a baby who had blissfully slept through her performance. And why shouldn't he, being privy to that voice on a daily basis.

The prison choir, which had sat demurely in the pews on the right side of the church, book-ended by their armed guards, now filed into the choir stall to perform. The first song was led by a small, burly young woman, with a charismatic smile that lacked a front tooth. "My mother drug me," she began to immediate laughter and applause. Her mother, it soon became clear, drug her to church, introducing her "to the only drug that will see you through." The congregation quickly joined her in the refrain, "You don't have to sniff it through your nose, shoot it in your veins." She left the choir stall and wandered down the aisles. Men and women reached out to take her hand.

She touched a weeping woman tenderly on the shoulder. I know physical contact is stringently controlled in prison, and also for women in the choir, so these gestures felt both illicit and totally natural, generous. For the members of the church were responding to her out of their own pain, and she was clasping their hands, touching their arms in simple consolation.

Listening to a recording of the service later, the voice that echoes even more achingly than that visual image, as achingly as that old man's refrain, "I know nothing, nothing," is the sound of another young woman singing "There's an army rising up to break every chain. . ." Every time her voice rises, the chorus made of choir and congregation lifts also to surround and steady it, singing with her "break ever chain, break every chain," freeing her to reach again. Listening, I experience the keenest sorrow and relief as if my own deepest need is known and met.

As I was leaving the church, an usher smiled at me and shook my hand saying, "We thank you for coming, Warden."

"It was an amazing experience," I assured him, smiling and hurrying down the stairs. I wanted to turn back and add *transcendent*—as if that might erase the misperception, if indeed that was what it was—as if the two realities couldn't, didn't, even at that moment coexist.

To See as I See

During the last year, a small local museum here held an interesting show, Optic Chiasm, about "the art of vision and science of sight." In one room, the show displayed posters of people with various visual disorders that included their photos and statements as well as images simulating the world as they might see it. In the other room, there were various tactile paintings incorporating braille, beautiful photographs of diseases of the retina and optic nerve, and also three large, brilliantly colored pointillist paintings made by a painter, Alan Eddy, now in his late thirties.

When Eddy was in his mid-twenties, at the beginning of a successful career as a painter, he suffered meningitis that left him almost completely blind, an unusual consequence of the disease, which more commonly damages the auditory nerve. He was told by eye doctors that he would be blind, but he discovered that he had retained some sight, an irregular sliver of vision in a different area in each eye as well as some color distinction. In the years that followed, he had found a way, working within these stringent visual constraints, to continue to paint. Drawing on his years of formal training, his formidable determination, and his love for his material and his art, these paintings were the result.

There was also a lecture series associated with the show. After the opening lecture by the curator, I was introduced to Eddy by his companion for the evening, with a casual, "I'm sure she has questions she would like to ask you." He turned to me expectantly. His eyes were unusually bright. With such a limited field of vision, I wondered aloud, how did he get a sense of overall composition and, more particularly, a feeling of aesthetic closure? He told me he'd come to realize rather recently that the compositions of the large-scale paintings he made now were very like those in small drawings he had made early in his career, before his illness. He also had a keen visual memory, in particular a memory for color, so he could envision the effect of combinations of colors his eyes were no longer able to detect. His palette was set up as a color wheel, so he knew almost without looking where the colors he needed were located. Pointillism allowed him to set the paint exactly within the small slivers of vision remaining to him.

I came away from the conversation with a sense of a numinous personality, someone completely absorbed in an activity that gave his life order and meaning and profound pleasure, It was amazing to me that he never considered giving up painting, turning to more plastic and tactile forms of art such as sculpture. Instead, from the moment he learned of his loss of sight, he had begun an intensive program of retraining his hand to his inner eye, his eye to what slipped through the sliver of sight he still had.

Allan Eddy gave the closing lecture of the series. It was clear that the purity of his focus had the same impact on the other members of the audience that it had on me, exhilarating and also chastening. I still had one last question for him that had come to me because of our earlier conversation. So in the question and answer session, I asked: "We create for ourselves as our first audience, but we also create to share our sense of beauty and order and affect with others. When we look at our work, we are also looking at is as others might see it. How do you understand this process when you can't see your works as others see them?"

He held absolutely still for a moment. I began to regret the question.

"It's been fourteen years I've been painting again—and it is only now I'm ready to admit that other people will never be able to see what I see."

His answer still reverberates with me. I wonder what I am, what we all are missing. I try to approximate it holding the flat of my hand close to my extended thumb, musing on that fine sliver of world. I sense something in there—still, luminous, a state where color obeys its own laws and our hearts do too. What, I wonder, would he have lost by accepting the world's constraints and not persisting, against such odds, in the creative use of his own?

)()()(

The poems, memoirs and stories we accepted (all of which responded to one or the other of the three main questions in the call) also fell upon reading and rereading into five categories that represent other interesting dimensions of the subjective experience of creativity—and of some of the literature about creativity. We have organized them in relation to these additional dimensions, which I discuss here.

I. Genesis

Where does the urge to create come from and what *is* it? Before the Enlightenment, rather than being thought of as a personal capability, an act of will, creativity was understood as an experience of discovery, revelation, receptivity. Awe was part of it, a sense of being joined to something larger and more powerful, so was gratitude. For many artists, these remain compatible ways of describing their experience.

The developmental psychologist and psychoanalyst Daniel Stern in his discussion of how identity is formed in infancy writes at some length in his book *The Interpersonal World of the Infant* about the earliest stage of self awareness which he names the emergent self. In this first stage, which takes place in the first two months after birth, the infant participates in the first exciting intimations of pattern. We are, above anything else, consciously pattern-seeking, pattern-needing creatures. To have a sense of ourselves as organisms, we need to relate our senses to consciousness. As the neural patterns made by moving a leg, hearing a voice, or turning a head, are discovered and rediscovered, our first amorphous neuronal buzz slowly becomes shaped, contained. We have a part in that shaping, come to know ourselves through it as, delighted, we keep returning to experiences that become progressively more reliable, more organized, more anticipated, inviting us to even greater explorations, greater integrations of sense and consciousness and action.

The making of art brings us, as do many other forms of creative flow, to a similar state—which is both the most primal of experiences and the most vast and mysterious, existential. Thomas Aquinas defines three essential elements of a work of art: integrity, harmony, and radiance. These are also qualities of every unique self-organizing, self-knowing being. This last quality, radiance, expresses that profound pleasure that we take in the perception of a self-organized form, a pleasure that speaks to something equally surprising and shapely inside us.

In the first section we hear many ways that poets play with these exploratory states—immediately sensuous and mysterious, discovered and initiated, randomly associated and integral—and with their meanings.

"Something wants to be said . . . /Something you don't want to say wants to be said," Claudia Van Gerven writes.

"I would have taken one more day/to think it through—" Ruth Silin archly admonishes in "This World."

"I am trying on binocular and monocular hyperspectral visionary eyes./I see more than I can tell you about that. I just want you to see./ I am sorting through piles of eyes trying to unseparate light from dark," Hannah Thomassen explains in "Opticality."

While Vida Cross in "The Night" expands the patterns we can make from sensory experience, speaking directly and at cross purposes: "This night is black./ Even blacker when things are in it."

A meditation, a feeling state Kathryn Machan expands in "All My People Dead": "deepest craving to survive/beyond blown clouds, a black horizon/ where words don't matter at all."

Bill Vernon, in "Rhythms" approaches the experience more mystically:

> I witnessed the fall flocks of starlings doing a similar thing, turning in waves undulating with wind and one will. I saw a thousand fishes, hanging on currents, turning in unison, contracting, expanding, and turning again, with sea weeds waving like large batons around them. Did all things but humans hear a natural music?

II. Female & Fertile

A number of writers, both male and female, explored how being female influences our experience of creativity, our opportunities to practice it, and how society's definition of both the feminine and the creative factor into women's definition of themselves as women and as artists.

Here we experience some of the dimensions of creativity as understood by social psychologists such as Mihaly Csikszentmihalyi and Howard Gardner. These researchers see creativity as more socially determined and defined. Creativity is making something novel and useful as defined by the surrounding society. Creativity takes place within domains of socially constructed knowledge that define intellectual or artistic disciplines. An artist, in the development of her art, is in dialogue with the artists who have come before her, the consensus, often unconscious, about what is the appropriate subject matter, the styles and genres, the techniques and intent of artistic activity.

Obviously, the definition of the domain in many art forms has changed dramatically in the last fifty years as more women and minorities have joined these conversations, however relative valuations may be slower to change. Whether a work is defined as creative is determined by what Gardner and Csikszentmihalyi call the field—the consensual opinion of contemporary cultural gatekeepers, that complex of critics, publishers, gallery owners, employers, fellow practitioners, and audience who ascribe cultural value. For example, since the rise of the novel in the nineteenth century, women have found it a compatible form, one in which their sense of form and subject matter matches readily with the 'common' reader. However, this popularity and accessibility can work against them when critics with a preference for the abstract, the emotionally detached, the stylized (in other words, for works that require a field of experts to interpret them) are in a position to define relative cultural worth.

For many aspiring and practicing artists, particularly women, their most influential field is and often remains their intimate circle—parents, spouses, children, friends. Within this circle there can be a struggle between the functional needs of these roles, which emphasize other-attentiveness, and the work of an artist, which requires inner direction and the ability to stay focused, what Csikszentmihalyi describes as an autotelic personality, one who does something primarily for inner reward not for social demand.

These themes are heard throughout this section, which opens with a number of poems directed toward young girls with artistic aspirations. All the poets, male and female, have a sense of the additional obstacles these young women face in finding themselves reflected in the domain itself (Paul Hostovsky's "Works for Trumpet"), or supported in their aspirations by the conditions around them (as in Jim Govoni's "Ice Skates and Piano Lessons").

The tension between motherhood and artistic drive plays out differently for different women at different points in their lives. Deborah Bacharach finds having a child makes her "a *charged* writer," now able to write anywhere and anytime. Maureen Flannery conceals the need she has for her own words, her own staff of life, as she kneads bread for her family. Deborah Pratt Curtiss in her memoir "Going Naked" describes how she has struggled both as an artist and now as a writer with how to define the powerful inner drive that impels her to follow her own vision. Is it brattiness or artistic integrity? Pat Barone's story "Rising and Falling" contrasts the concerns of an aging poet mother fully devoted to her art and a middle-aged daughter who seeks a richer balance between her drives as an artist and a mother.

III. Artistic Process

The pleasure of artistic process, at its best, is found in Csikszentmihalyi's description of the flow state: ". . . being fully involved in an activity for its own sake. The ego falls away. Time flies. Every action, movement, and thought follows inevitably from the previous one, like playing jazz. Your whole being is involved and you're using your skills to the utmost."

Flow is a state reminiscent of that sense of the emergent self described by Daniel Stern, where action and understanding constantly reinforce each other. An analogous account of the artistic process is found in Kenneth Wright's *Mirroring and Attunement: Self-Realization in Psychoanalysis and Art.* Wright builds on Stern and, in his description of the role of the art object for both viewer well as artist, describes well its relational nature:

> One of the things that determines our judgement of a work of art is the degree to which we experience it as having relevance—by which I mean resonance with the shapes and forms of our own feeling. A work of art is successful in this sense, when it mirrors our own 'forms of feeling.' In fulfilling this function, it repeats in some measure for the viewer what it performed for the artist in the course of its creation. In the same way that the 'shapes' the artist fashioned were the living substantiation of his emotional being, so for the viewer who now relates to them they become something he can inhabit, and through which he is enabled to become more fully himself.

The Canadian psychologist Liane Gabora extends this idea in several ways. She sees the role of creativity in general to be a remodeling of the worldview of an individual.

She describe the healing purpose of creative constructions for the creator—whether painting or novel or theory or invention:

> *Just as the body heals itself when wounded, elements of a 'body of knowl-edge' modify each other to solve problems, reduce dissonance, or accommodate unexpected events . . . . Most thoughts have little effect on a worldview, but the occasional thought triggers another, which triggers an 'avalanche' of conceptual changes, resulting in a massive restructuring of knowledge.*

Creative people, she suggests, are more highly sensitive to these shifts. "Creative individuals wrestle with issues or ideas that are, for them, ill-defined, or in a state of potentiality, which become well-defined in the process of considering them from different perspectives, or contexts."

She also sees these perturbations and the consequent remodeling as encouraging increasingly complex and resilient stages of organization—sees creativity as playing a cultural role, increasing a society's resilience as well.

Art reshapes a mental universe, but it is also densely, inextricably materialistic as well. With writing, unlike the visual and plastic arts, the material used is language, a common symbol system, quintessentially social, public. It comes to us well-worn. It can cage or liberate us. Imposed or thoughtlessly appropriated, it can divorce us from what is unique in our own experience. The struggle for writers is to make words reflect their subjective universe, to connect them with what is fresh, novel, in their own perception, emotion, and thought.

Although writers struggle to make a common language reflect their most intimate reality, they also find that hard sought, hard fought language can trap them in the habitual and will use artificial constraints to surprise themselves into something novel, truer—using new forms, sonnet or sestina, a new point of view. "We carry our own atmosphere, a thin/ Slick of warmth and wet," Laurence Snydal writes in his poem "Wind Chill Factor." "The same glaze surrounds my cherished thinking," he continues. It precludes as much as it protects.

The poems in this section all evoke different dimensions of the dialogue going on between an artist and her or his process. We feel it in Diane Giardi's "In the Studio" as she describes the tension between intent and accident in her work. "This week I'm convinced they're good for each other/ . . . Last week I cried I would forever keep them apart."

For Jo Going it is the use of an intentional constraint—like painting in subzero conditions—that leads to flow, a release from "the small self/ scratching, muddletating."

Don Thackrey finds that liberation in the strict demands of the sonnet form. Hostovksy and Thomassen, ignoring Marianne Moore's definition of poetry as imaginary gardens with real toads in them, provide us with incompletely imagined poems with real cats on them.

The two stories included in this section explore the cascade of thoughts that come when an artist's understanding of his or her own process is unexpectedly challenged, bringing an entire worldview into question. The artist in Joel Wachman's "The Ownership of Desire" begins to understand what it might mean not to have, as she does, the capacity to subsume one's rawest and most destructive drives in one's work: "She wanted to understand, but could not reach across that chasm. . . . Until you look closely, so closely you can see all of the details, the connective tissue that holds one part to another, you remain strangers."

J. J Steinfeld's artist in "Past Artistry" finds that his entire understanding of his artistic process may be resting on false premises:

> *I'm miserable when I'm not painting, terrified of the unproductive periods,*
> *so I do anything to keep working. Over seven hundred canvases completed in the*
> *last thirty years, not counting all the sketches and drawings and other artistic*
> *projects I've done. All related to what had happened. To not knowing.*

Tim Leskiw's essay explores what happens when we intentionally upend our formal assumptions, step out of our comfort zone, try to write fiction, for example, when our home base is non-fiction. He ends up with a greater appreciation of his own process and its relation to his worldview and sensibility: "A veil's been lifted. We've glimpsed—and in doing so, been woven into—a vast and mysterious world-wide tapestry, if only for a few hours."

IV. Artists' Lives

The role of artist is both a creative support and a constraint to the artist. It provides a social role and the expectations that accompany that role, but it also stylizes the experience, flattens it and distorts. This is a dimension of creativity and constraint that lends itself more to story, and satire, since it is about the discrepancy between appearances and reality, between what we really are and how we want to see ourselves and be seen.

In "Stars of the Startups," Michele Markarian plays with attitudes about the day job, which is both so necessary to most artists and so difficult for them to assimilate into their vision of themselves as 'pure' artist. Mike Maggio in

"Atelier" takes the point of view of the model who placidly survives the artist's gaze, "collecting herself from about the room like a schoolgirl collecting leaves." Alan Swyer in "The Oracle" describes the dance for control—of images, of worldview—between a filmmaker and the new-age prophet who is commissioning his film.

V. Life . . . Art . . . Life

Gabara sees the continuing creative process of upheaval and reorganization as a way of developing greater conceptual fluency and complexity of organization as individuals and as cultures. The Chinese artist and social activist Ai Weiwei echoes this:

> *I realize a piece of art cannot change the political or social conditions of the world directly. But I myself change when I participate in these conditions. I gain an understanding of the relationship between my art and society. It helps me feel grounded in the creative process. I am not seeking to create complete or perfect works. I am doing what I must do*
> .

In the last section of this anthology, our creative conversation with the world around us and with the worlds that art creates are both the focus.

Céline Keating describes her quest to locate the real world of Louise Penny's novels. Michael Hess finds creative sanctuary in a location that defies his earlier expectations:

> *I have actually grown quite comfortable with this world, reconciled myself to the horror and beauty that lurks under the surfaces and in the interiors of all the places that I inhabit. I am so comfortable with this world that I did not flinch when the black flies hatched a few weeks later and infested my new writing space with their glorious buzz and bite.*

In Michael Onofrey's "Klimt" a house painter befriends a woman who has lost a daughter in war. They both describe how attention to something outside themselves—for him, the impersonal flow of people, for her, the heat and grit of a day alone in the desert—brings their inner worlds into a new equilibrium, an engagement with physical reality that begins to make the inconceivable bearable.

The narrator in J.J. Steinfeld's "A Life of Books" begins to make space for a new life for himself by ridding himself of his most prized possessions, his books. He whimsically gifts any stray passer-by with both a book and the key turning point in his life inextricably enfolded into his experience of reading it.

Anna Steegmann in her three short essays explores the world that exists between the two languages, German and English, that have shaped her life. We glimpse both the relief of having these languages communicate as she translates her favorite German author into English, an interchange that clarifies her own aspirations as a writer—and her anguish at what it means to rest in the silence that defines the new land in which without warning she finds herself, the land of grieving, where no language suffices.

In this cycling between the delightful surprise and raw shock of life and the at times arduous and at other times effortless transmutations of art, the reality of death remains the most powerful invitation to create, to reclaim what is most uniquely and universally our own. John Sibley Williams expresses this well in his poem "Terminus":

> *It makes no difference if the answers are born*
> *of imagination or dust.*
> *However it ends, the moment before I'll still be*
> *a curious specimen homed in a body at least I tried to explain.*

We hope you find some of your own experiences with creativity and constraint echoed here, especially those moments when these concepts mysteriously meld, pull apart, mutate into their opposite, and we know them to be, like the clear glass surface and silvered back of a mirror, equally essential to our understanding of ourselves and of the world around us.

Note:

Although Stern in later work distances himself from this emergent dimension of the developing self, it has been picked up by James W. Fowler in his discussion of religious development and faithful change is so highly descriptive of a central dimension of artistic creativity that I discuss it here.

Sources:

Aerts, D., Broekaert, J. and Gavora, L. "Intrinsic Contextuality as the Crux of Consciousness." In K.Yasue, ed., *Fundamental Approaches to Consciousness.* Tokyo: John Benjamin, 1999.

Brougher, Kerry. "Reconsidering Reality: An Interview with Ai Weiwei." In Hirschorn and Mori Art Museums, ed., *Ai Weiwei: According to What?* New York: Prestel Publishing, 2012. Pp. 38-43.

Csikszentmihalyi, Mihaly. *Creativity: Flow and the Psychology of Discovery and Invention.* New York: Basic Books, 1998.

Fowler, James W. *Faithful Change: The Personal and Public Challenges of Postmodern Life.* Nashville: Abingdon Press, 1996.

Gabora, L. "Cognitive Mechanisms Underlying the Creative Process." In T. Hewett and T. Kavanaugh, eds., *Proceedings of the Fourth International Conference on Creativity and Cognition,* October 13-16, Loughborough University, U.K.. Pp. 126-133.

Gardner, Howard. "Creators: Multiple Intelligences." In Karl H. Pfenninger and Valerie R. Shubik, eds. *The Origins of Creativity.* Oxford: Oxford University Press, 2001. Pp. 117-143.

Kaufman, James C. *Creativity 101.* New York: Springer, 2009.

Stern, Daniel. *The Interpersonal World of the Infant: A View from Psychoanalysis and Developmental Psychology.* New York: Basic Books, 1985, 2000.

Stokes, Patricia D. *Creativity from Constraints: The Psychology of Breakthrough.* New York: Springer, 2006.

Truitt, Anne. *Daybook: The Journal of an Artist.* New York: Penguin, 1982.

Wright, Kenneth. *Mirroring and Attunement: Self Realization in Psychoanalysis and Art.* New York: Routledge, 2009.

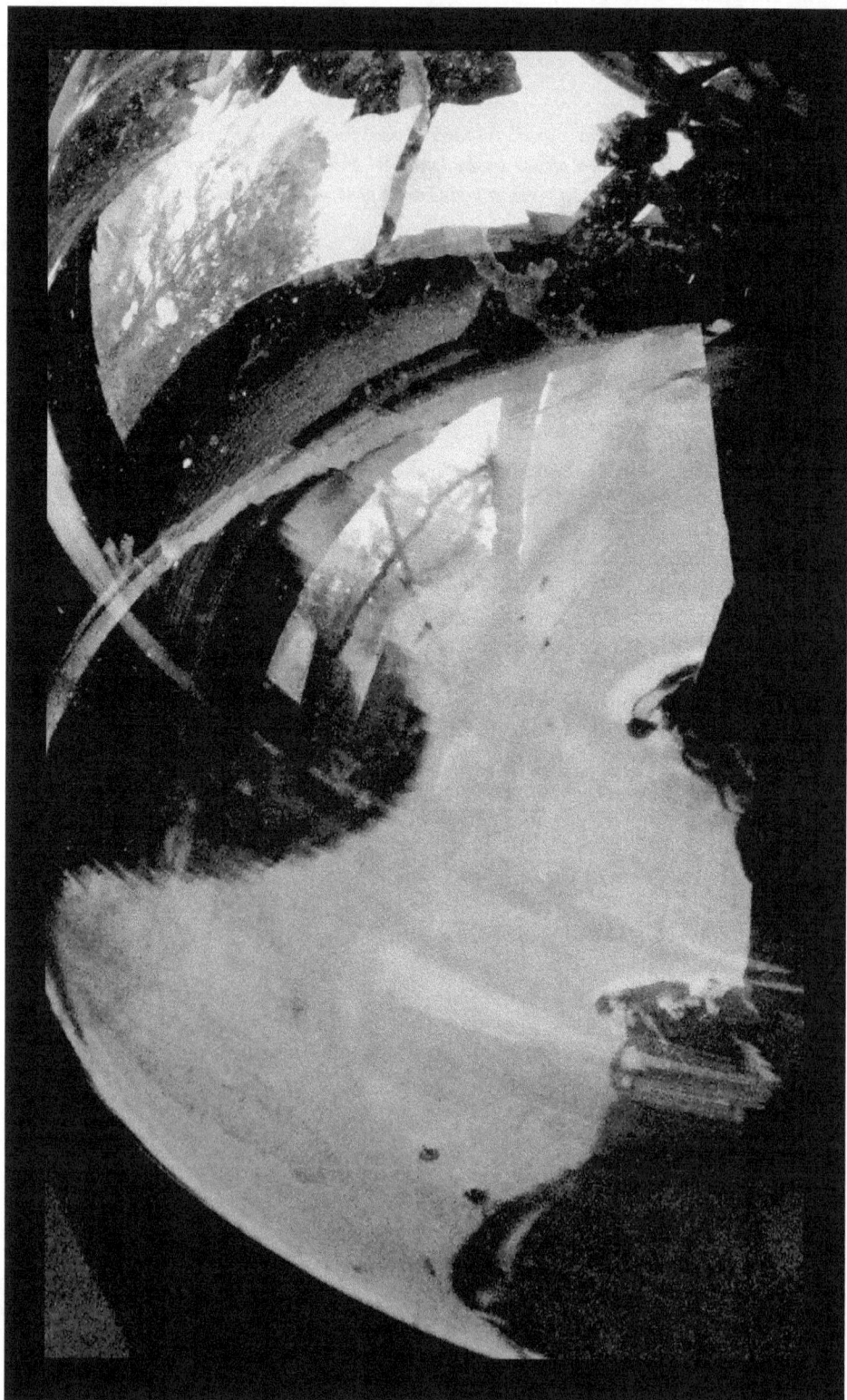

I
GENESIS

CLAUDIA VAN GERVEN

SOMETHING WANTS TO BE SAID

Squadron of wide-winged
pelicans trolling the trough
white squall of gulls exploding.
There's a pebbled shore, tide pool stink:

rot of life, life of rot. That story.

And you want it all to be
orange sprays, white organdy
Princess Grace in her oasis
of veils. Prince coiffed, plausible
in his Principality of Sand—
then fiery finale. That story.

Or something simple as bread, yeast-giddy

crust broken, knife smearing
clot of butter, see-through
sweetness of strawberries
crushed with sugar.

You don't want to taste coppery sea tang

in the back of your throat,
penny licked as a child
the slaughter of the wheat
silos stuffed with subsidies
oceans between us
and what we feed on

Something you don't want to say wants to be said

raving mad in the back of your throat.
Your muscled heart keeps
its faithful resolve, red salted
tides declaring your life again
while the rose climbs the trellis
opens her lovely, red mouths

RUTH MARGOLIN SILIN

THIS WORLD
(if it were up to me)

I would not have made it so.
I would have taken one more day to
think it through—and if it came to pass
that I erred on one small thing or another,
then the blame would be my own—and
when they whispered my name in silent prayer,
"Oh, God, Yahweh, Jesus, Allah, Jehovah, Shiva—
hear my words" . . . I would reply:
figure it out folks, I cannot do it all.

Why so much space for water I ponder,
when nearby earth is parched and scarce?
A little equity here and there takes care of that.
Now, do men—and women I hasten to add—truly
require mountains to climb and conquer?
To what purpose? Most difficult when
burying the dead.
And there is the matter of all those skins with
varying shades of white and black and brown.
I am most clear on this—ONE shade for all.
Perhaps a lovely violet or maybe golden amber to
reflect the honey I offer as a gift—maybe the shade
of blush that Eve displays when first she sees
the Man and tries to cover up her startling parts.
Nowhere in sight would I place an apple or
a serpent to confuse.

I know I would make massive hills of golden daffodils
and never a fence—for there is no one likes a fence.
I would carve a cave or two for certain bears who like
to hibernate—decide how many beasts of burden to
fill this world—ponder size and limits for all
matter of inhabitants.
I should make no borders, no dividing lines
between the rivers and the forests, no maps,
no conquerors to say what's mine and what is
yours and later have another come along and
change it all again.
So simple when what is yours is mine and what
is mine is yours. Socialism, communism, democracy,
autocracy, royalty and all that ilk, would count
for naught for there would be enough to go around.
Civility as commonplace as breathing—we would surely
love our neighbors as ourselves.
Obesity would not exist, eliminating
weight-loss clinics and fitness centers.
Why treadmills when human gait on grass
and earth is so efficient?
One's teeth would last throughout one's life
along with guarantees for knees and hips.
I am still working on the common cold and other
bodily matters, simple and complex, but these
may take another hour or two.

I will surely add spiked rainbows between the stars
so all may look to Heaven to review my work,
and, yes, Virginia, Heaven is ensured.
Finally, sweet language of the poets shall be our words,
"Utopia" our name.

But this I know before I start,
I would not have made it so.

PATRICK HANSEL

AT THE END OF THE 6TH DAY

My fingers stub on Adam's clay
and I roll him over sage and mint

to flower his skin. He looks rough.
This man-making taxes me.

I should have birthed him out of water,
clear, moving, washing my hands as I worked,

or better still, from sky, all and nothing
in the same breath, unbound, like me.

But no, I chose dirt, the hardest earth,
something you get stuck in. And now

my hands have fingers thick as roots,
my mind takes on heart. I have become blood

to him, and I must breathe. This is the only
one I will send away with a task;

the only creature I will name
before he is awake.

PAUL HOSTOVSKY

MERTON

There was Merton the monk—the poet—and then there was Merton
the kid in my high school class who got caught screwing his girlfriend
in the dark auditorium, behind the thick green curtain. They were
doing it on the stage when the vice principal busted them.
Imagine, the vice principal of all people, entering stage left.
What was he doing skulking around back there in the dark
auditorium anyway, Merton with his pants around his ankles
was probably wondering, and is still probably wondering today,
the way a really good poem can echo over a lifetime. The girl's
skirt was hiked up above her waist, and her shining dark nipples
shone even in the dark, as the vice principal passed ominously
in front of the pale moon of Merton's bare and pumping butt.

Merton the monk had a brother—not a monastic brother, a real
brother, a biological younger brother who is given only
a paragraph in *The Seven Story Mountain*. Imagine, a paragraph
out of all those pages given to God. But I don't think they're related—
I mean I don't think the profligate Merton of my high school in New Jersey
is the brother of the celibate Merton of that monastery in Kentucky,
the one who wrote lots of poetry. I mean *lots* of poetry. Maybe even
too much poetry. Because there is such a thing as being profligate
with poetry, writing too much and too often. And here is where
they may have been related, Merton the monk and Merton the mendicant
begging the vice principal (with the girlfriend buttoning up beside him)
not to tell. Imagine the vice principal not telling, simply turning

around, tactfully exiting stage left, and leaving the two
young lovers to themselves, his clicking footsteps echoing
across the silent, dark auditorium, letting them carry on
where they left off—open-mouthed, speechless with

surprise and delight, and pleasure. And how could they not
pick up the thread, pull on it some more? And how could he not
pick up the pen, and write the next poem, Merton the monk, the poet
exulting in the poem whose thread he was just itching to tear
out of himself? And how could we not imagine the vice principal
not telling anyone, returning to his office, perhaps a little flushed,
sitting down at his desk, staring a long time at the photo of his wife,
a sexy smile playing at her lips some game of its own imagining?

HANNAH THOMASSEN

OPTICALITY

> *. . . an image does not act for what it*
> *shows, but for the questions it raises.*
> —*Lacan*

I am trying to see 360 degrees with my back to the moon.
I am trying to explain multifaceted vision,
spin gold into words. I am running a footrace
with dementia, trying to make words do their work.
I am trying to drive through the rain in the snow
so I know where to go now and next.

I am trying to look death in the eye,
convert light through an adjustable assembly of lenses.
I don't want to be in over my head.

I am trying to find the right page, the right eye
and the left. Trilobites had crystals for eyes.
Jumping spiders have one large simple eye
and many small eyes, would that help?
I need more retina display. 360% more density and pixels.
But is that upgrade too large to load?

I am trying on binocular and monocular hyperspectral visionary eyes.
I see more than I can tell you about that. I just want you to see.
I am sorting through piles of eyes trying to unseparate light from dark.

PETRA DAI WALECH

THE FISH-EYE DOOR

It is a safe place I am told
It is a tight place I am told
It is a small space I am told

There is one door—and one eye that sees all.

The fish-eye door.

It has seen men to the darkest places our waters know
and seen the brightest sun after the deep journey.

It has heard the siren's call
and it has heard the worst silence of all.

It has been to the birth place of species long gone
remembered only by dehydrated bones.

The submarine door is made of steel—
all the breathing beings depend on the air-tight seal.

The red light blinks every three seconds
by the forty-third blink all is a pulse.

I try to time my breath to the pulsing
but I try in vain, my lungs fail to sustain.

There is a sign below the eye
It reminds me to be safe.

I keep my focus on the fish-eye.

I blink first but I am not too disappointed
this eye does not know what it is to close.

The light seizes and there is an alarm.

Grab the polyurethane arms holding my sides to the floor:

Grab the walls

Grab the floor

Grab the seat in front

I can see it
But I need a map to find the door.

If death were a journey
it would be through the fish-eye I would travel.

Through the fish-eye I would drown.

The breath of the vessel,
Processed in a propane tank and sanitized from steam.

It is screaming and it finds my ears taken off guard.

My stomach and the submarine drop
in a synchronized fall.

Red light washes into my retinas.

Alexander on a white horse
washed away with red;

Caesar's laurel leaf crown
washed away with red;

Attila and the Huns
washed away with red;

Erikson abreast great ships
washed away with red.

Froth bubbles filled with fear
or arrogance or carbon monoxide quiet while it kills.

And I ask myself what they thought while they bled out.

While their power seeped from their pores—

And their expectations outgrew their reign—

And they found their titles too tight—

And they found it hard to breath with the lungs they were given.

And I find that I was lied to.

And I scream but the siren is louder—And I am running but the floor drops
faster—And I breathe but the air is thinner—And I reach but the door is
farther—
           I remember being a child in an elevator

                                        and how it felt falling . . .

VIDA CROSS

THE NIGHT

This night is black

Even blacker when things are in it

The house across the street is a
black house

The car resting in the yard is a
black car

The man on his front stoop is a
black man

He feels the air on his face
a soft touch

A lightning bug runs into his cheek
he sees
black wings

He checks his breathing

If he can breathe in air
nothing is near

Once the air feels used
murky
stiff
something's there
he tells himself

A door opens
his face turns

He sucks in his last gulp
holds his breath
then smells the alcohol
on his skin
the cigarette smoke on his clothes

He sees his dark daughter
lightly chasing
the even darker firefly

Minor troubles
they
favored a mother
who'd died inside
when her daughters were born

His little girl danced around him
around the car
through the dark yard

He figured he was
invisible
too dark
too drunk
to be seen

Seated
eyes half closed
so he was almost gone

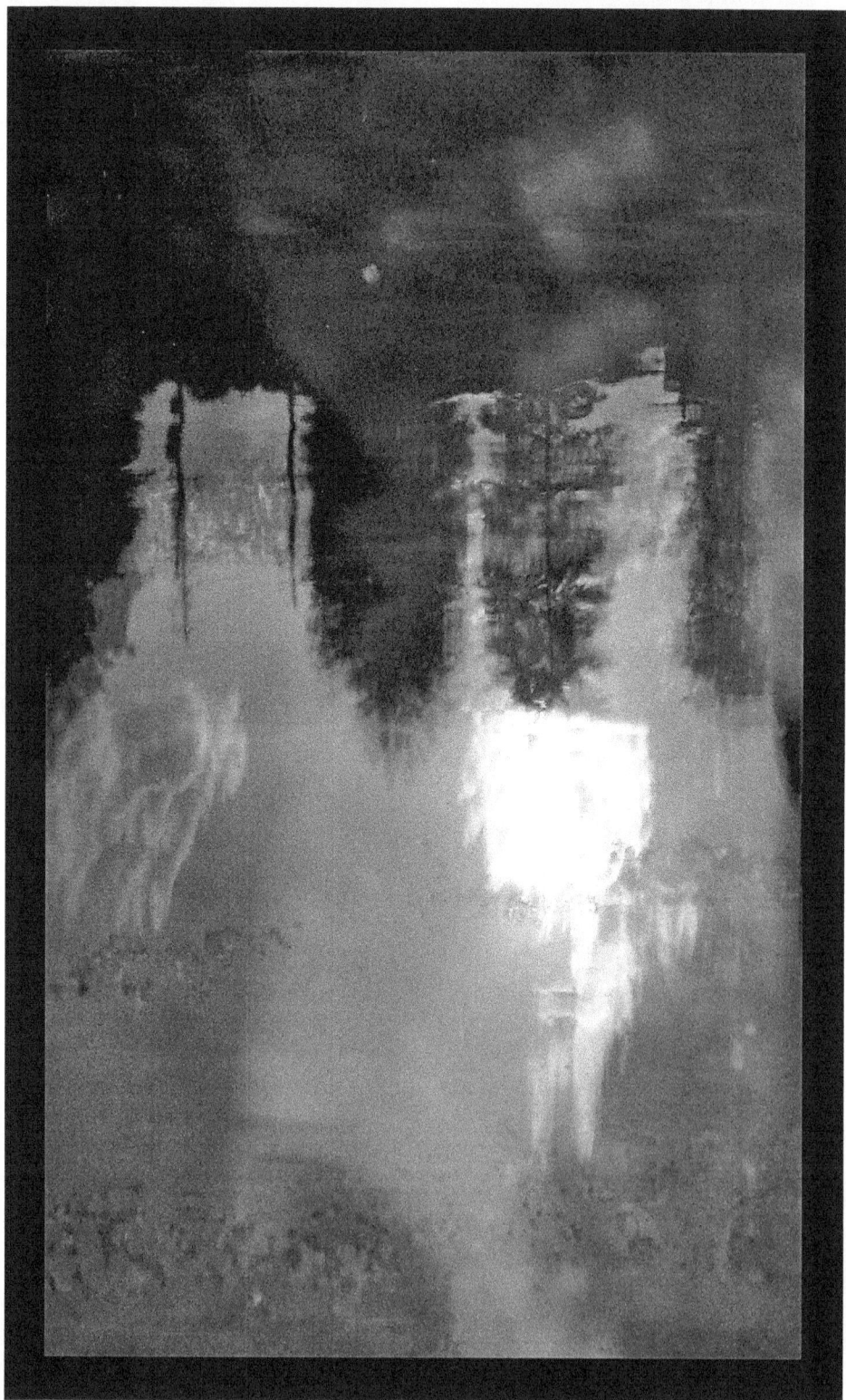

KATHARYN HOWD MACHAN

WITH ALL MY PEOPLE DEAD

why should I think about a poem?
And yet I do, it standing there,
vulnerable at the edge of shore,
one leg crooked up and humbly
bending its long lines toward blue
water where a frog might wait
beneath the whirr and dash of fast
thin dragonflies, calm where an image
might reach and close to satisfy
sharp hunger, deepest craving to survive
beyond blown clouds, a black horizon
where words don't matter at all.

IRA SCHAEFFER

CICADA

Strange how we both fell
from the scarred tree,
then hid underground
latched to the taproot.
But you broke the spell,
reversed the wedge
blooming strange
and beautiful
with the red voices of night.

Tonight your frenzied voice
shrieks the darkness alive, while I
sputter here in a blood trance,
trying to rise
with the tune
that spins the earth.

I want to believe
inside this crust of skin
a pure flame tremors,
like the sunlight's unfolding
or the trembling of stars.
But this cinch of bones and brain
squeezes me. I feel the sky
shutting, or is it my body
turning to stone?

Now my breath flickers, edging
to the light—behind the glass
inside this shell—I know
each muffled cry
dies with fire—
this is the way—I must
come back alive—this
is the way of burning.

BILL VERNON

RHYTHMS

The world seemed like a whirl around me, and though I moved through it confidently, without hesitation, things began to stick in my mind. Persistent afterimages. I didn't understand why they kept appearing. Like most kids, I lived in the present.

Eventually, I considered them signs of life's complexity, its depth and richness. But that seemed too much like concluding with what I hoped was true. My mind like a dog would dig up and chew at the memories. Like in the Golden Lamb, the oldest hotel in Ohio, where I daily delivered five newspapers to stack on the counter for guests: one day I watched hotel workers shove three grandfather clocks into place so their pendulums jerked, the hours boomed discordantly, and their ticking tocked enough to unsettle my nerves and chase me away. A week later, delivering papers, I noticed their pendulums were arcing in concert, their ticking and announcing of times were almost exactly the same.

This elated me and seemed to prove my first understanding. I began noticing other things, like while sitting on a porch at dusk, how the fireflies sporadically glowing climbed from bushes and grass, but then later, in full dark, most of them were flashing together.

I witnessed the fall flocks of starlings doing a similar thing, turning in waves undulating with wind and one will. I saw a thousand fishes, hanging on currents, turning in unison, contracting, expanding, and turning again, with sea weeds waving like large batons around them. Did all things but humans hear a natural music?

Then I sensed myself doing it too, carrying *The Middletown Journal* in a canvas bag on my bike, dropping copies at doors, single-mindedly creating a route and a need, talking with customers until some became friends. I knew four other kids doing the same thing with other newspapers in my hometown alone.

Those visions came with me into the city my first year of high school, so I felt myself repeating them while walking in crowds, letting the people pull me along, stopping at crossings, rushing on, swirling towards doors, parting at obstacles. With hundreds I listened to a concert, applauded, rose and shouted Encore! Ole!

I was comforted by my understanding until my father died. Then I dreamed of a sky darkened with feathers and heard the wings of passenger pigeons roaring like motors. I stood aside and heard the thunder of buffalo, felt the ground shake, saw the dark brown backs rushing over rolling hills from horizon to horizon. And beneath the lights of a passing jet, beneath the moon and the fire of stars, I also walked among bones below the cliffs they ran off of.

People like other things ended. How many had lived here before me? Now I was aware of the dangers. What held us together also pushed us toward an edge that I would probably not see until I felt myself falling.

II
FEMALE & FERTILE

ROSEMARY VOLZ

GIRL POET

She will learn to commune with her own heart,
To squander time beautifully,
To contemplate light falling on objects
And the space between words.
Although she can't properly pronounce
The minor rivers of Europe,
She will be nobody's muse.

She will understand the texture of things,
The veneer of the world,
And the underbelly of the beast.
She will know what is art
And what is just pretending
And know she has no right to know.

She will accumulate a stack of shiny bricks
And never find a landscape that suits her.

One day while separating the excellent from the ordinary
A shadow will fall upon the girl
And she will sense that the ordinary is closer to heaven
And her life will never be easy.
Still, she will pray for a rebirth of wonder.

On the eighth day she will sprinkle words on the kitchen table.
Unruly verbs will bounce off her coffee cup.
Complacent nouns will melt into the grain.
She will marvel at the infinite combinations
And their power to create love, thunder, and best of all, light.
She will learn to use human language with animal grace,
Then throw out the sentimental favorites and wait,
Wait for the flash to the heart, the lifting of the veil
And she will know—it is good.

RICHARD KING PERKINS II

FINDING HER MUSE

As she quietly lays in her crib,
no one can predict that this child
will become a doctor or accountant
with any certainty, even in a family
rich with doctors or accountants.

Tonight, she slumbers in the titian vapors
of untended potential where
every pathway is possible and alluring.
Change begins with stirring awareness
and the subtle stoking of what is missed.

Even at the breast,
her auspicious mist begins to dissipate.
The roads to Tripoli are eclipsed
while the streets of Denver hang brightly
across an otherwise lackluster horizon.

But would any have said
she will become a seeker of stars,
searching every night through
a magnificent telescope,
one that's never been trained
on the clearest of attainable skies?

JIM GOVONI

ICE SKATES AND PIANO LESSONS

On the third floor
in an unrefined Victorian
a young girl dreams
of ice skates and piano lessons.

With her eyes closed
soul open
she glides with dancer's grace
across a frozen pond
freeing piano melodies
blocked by the knot
of her narrow staircase.

Door slams . . . eyes open.

Father returns home
from emptying garbage into an open truck.
Mother remains in the back room
foot-pedaling her Singer
in endless rhythm
sewing up hope for others.

PAUL HOSTOVSKY

WORKS FOR TRUMPET

We are listening to Alison Balsom
play Bach. "Do we have to

listen to this?" Amber, eleven,
buckled up in the passenger seat,

balks, bucks. We're late for school—
her backpack, lunchbox, and violin

ride mutely in the back. She looks
down at the CD box, makes a face:

"Who is *Botch* anyway?"
Her violin leaps violently to the floor

as I brake for a stopped school bus.
"It's not *Botch*," I tell her. "It's *Bach*—

only the greatest musician who ever lived,
that's who." She gives the box a second,

closer look—"Bach is pretty. How old is Bach?"—
frowning at the photo of Alison Balsom

on the front cover. "That's not Bach," I tell her.
"It's Alison Balsom. On trumpet. And yes,

she *is* pretty." Amber raises her left eyebrow,
then stitches it to its twin. "A *girl*

playing the trumpet?" And I can hear
the wheels turning, tuning, inside her head

as the school bus trundles dumbly along
and I follow close behind. "There aren't

any girls who play trumpet in *my* school,"
she says. "Only boys." Alison belts out another

string of impossibly gorgeous arpeggios.
Amber looks out the window, scratches

her head. She is listening. I don't say
a word, pull in behind the school bus, park.

We sit there for a long time, the violin
on the floor, the trumpet in the air, Alison

Balsom breathing Bach, breathing beauty,
Amber late for school and listening hard.

HANNAH THOMASSEN

SEATTLE TRANSIT, circa 1962

In her dream of being
on the bus, from behind
and across from her I watch

her hair fluffed gold against
the window flashing city-bright—

Nordstrom's Shoes,
Fredrick & Nelson, Bon Marche.

She is on her way to forever,
does not know will never know
it is not the forever

she dreams, high-rise perspective
on the Sound, drafting table slanted

against the light, sharpened
pencils in a row, fog horn,

pills
she will no longer need

free at last
thank god almighty, rich
sexy, high, wide—

she is lost just now on the bus

dreaming up

that Star Wars Vanity
she is yet to build,

the Interior Architecture
Student Show
she will never see

having arrived by then
at forever

never
in this dream.

DEBORAH BACHARACH

FIRE, APHASIA, AND THE SPIRIT WORLD

I had a routine before starting to write. First, I'd read a couple pages of a mystery, or more than a couple. I'd check email, play some solitaire, and finally if I had fifteen minutes left before bedtime, I'd start counting syllables and considering line breaks.

Then I had a baby.

The first few weeks after Rose was born I would sit staked to the breastfeeding chair and feel a current through my limbs, vibrating deep inside. One night it felt like "I must have it. Take me now." Except it wasn't sex I wanted; it was writing. I've been calling myself a writer for fifteen years, I went to graduate school, I teach writing, and I never found this passion. I have no time for solitaire, very little time for the bathroom, but somehow, I have to write.

I feel like a faucet desperate to open. I'm the blue metal one outside. The handle sticks, and it's hard to get going, but you know when you're pressing at it, water is waiting to burst out. It's the water for the garden. It's not delicate. It doesn't have to be drawn up. It's power. It explodes out at the first opportunity.

I write when she's pulling the papers out of my to-do pile and putting them in the recycling bin. When she's fallen asleep in her stroller and she'd wake if I transferred her to the car, I sit on the cement curb of the parking lot, cars pulling in beside me, and write. When she's fallen asleep on the way home from shopping, I sit cramped in the front seat of the car, my notebook propped on the steering wheel and write. When she's asleep on my lap, and I can't reach the computer or a pen, I turn on the tiny tape recorder and whisper what I want to write. I step over her sleeping body to get to my computer and write. I write when I should be asleep. I write as though my life depended on it. Sometimes I think her life depends on it.

As I release her from the stroller because she is screaming, exhausted, refusing to sleep unless strapped to my chest, I feel my jaw clench. Clench like a socket wrench? The black pads on a bicycle? The search for words distracts me, releases me. I have never hit my child, never yanked her, slammed her, bashed her head against the bureau, thrown her from the second floor window. The words are all on the page and out of my body.

I keep a baby diary. It's full of the mundane arcana of our life: how many hours she sleeps, what foods she rejected this week. I want to remember this information, but this is not writing; it's recording. There's no heat in it. I keep writing until the words flare.

Every morning she wakes up next to me and after her morning ritual—nursing, flailing her arms so I'll pick her up, grinning at Daddy—I take a good look. Her face is a little rounder, or she has more chin, or less. I'm on high alert. I don't want to miss it as she tries her first Popsicle, the puckering quizzical look she gives me. I'm watching every second as she slowly squats, lifts a black pebble, and brings it closer and closer to her open mouth.

Rose is gorgeous, courageous, and clever, and she can say "uh oh" with great aplomb, but she doesn't sleep. Not nearly enough for my sanity. Sleep deprivation makes me miserable, but it's had two unforeseen advantages for my writing life: aphasia and visions.

She's taken away my ordinary words. I start to say "telephone" as in "please hand me the" and my lips won't go into the right shape. I'll either say "the thing that you hold against your ear for sound vibrations," "the sacrosanct totality," or I'll say "turnip." "Hop along" can mean I don't know where I've put the baby's white fluffy coat. It's disconcerting and annoying when I'm trying to grab the diaper bag and get out the door, but it's also magical. I'm constantly surprised. "Baby carrier" becomes "umbrella" becomes "monster." I know it has something to do with their rhythm and something to do with the way the carrier has straps that look like tentacles. I'm taking new routes around my brain.

As a writer, I've always tried to end up in unknown territory. I want to be surprised. Even more, I've always yearned for trance state, to be in that place where wild images just flow. I'm here now. I am so close to the spirit world; I just close my eyes and it comes. One day I saw a polka dotted Ferris wheel, mountains of burnished metal, and the tree from the Garden of Eden become an English hedge.

Surrealists play games; shamans go on fasts; I had a baby.

I didn't suddenly become an artist because of my daughter. But, I am a changed writer because of her. I am a *charged* writer. She threw open the doors to the furnace and blew coals into flame.

MAUREEN TOLMAN FLANNERY

HALF-BAKED

I have kneaded life's dough
with one hand only,
pressed its plumpness, folded its flour
back into itself again and again,
learning to delight in the honeyed yeast smell,
in the warm rolling of the outside inward
and the top back out to the bottom,
in the silken patina that comes
onto what was mucky and clung
to the knuckles, cuticles,
between the active fingers of that one hand,

at the same time
holding a pen to cross out words,
glutinous, glossy, leavened, viscous,
record the memory of fresh bread
in Grandmother's kitchen
or speculate as to how they regulated
the temperature of wood burning stoves
or allude to the way illness was baked out of the body
in the ancient Aztec oven called *temazcal*
or anticipate on paper
how evenly the bread would bulge
over the edges of the pan,
the lonely hand still pushing,
pressing, folding air in.

Always needing the poem
as I kneaded the dough,
I hoped my hungry family would not know
that the earth-brown crust
of the finished loaves mattered less
than the sound of my words.

ESSENCE

If you would find her,
do not search for her at home,
rushing inefficiently through labyrinthine days
that do not open to a palace courtyard,
hands in the toilet rinsing fetid flannel diapers,
her mind in ancient Egypt
(Isis with the Horus child,
piecing her dismembered spouse)
or reading poetry,
rafted thoughts riding white-water words
down brimming spring streams
while she's bedded beside a nursing baby
attached like suction dart to half her heart.

Seek her, instead, at night
while other sleepers free their souls
to solve the testy riddles waking consciousness cannot
or visit long departed parents to mend imperfect holidays.
There, as her frail sleepy body twitches
with the last withdrawal of wakefulness
her spirit slips away.
Only a seer will perceive the silver chord
that stretches from her form
to the bulging file beside the writing desk
where her essence wrestles with unfinished poems.

THE UNFINISHED PROJECT

Women, it seems, have this insatiable need
to amass the trappings of their craft—
whole closets stacked with rainbowed rows of quilting fabric,
fishing tackle boxes stocked
with beads of every conceivable shade,
basswood for carving, laces for trimming
the doll clothes she intends to make.

But the time and supplies never quite come out even.
Doesn't she usually die or take a lover
or have another child
before she tires of the thing she has learned to do so well.
Always a few projects, eagerly begun,
hang around the basement in boxes.

You see them at rummage sales
the needlepoint canvas abandoned mid-stitch,
whole boxes of cross-stitch floss
complete with pattern books
and sometimes a half-finished picture,
or a case containing squeezed-out oil paints
and a pallet crusted with globs of dry color.

Each neglected art
projecting itself to completion
strains toward a craved wholeness
with nostalgia for attention once received.
This need of the unmade thing to come to being
leans into a new woman
hoping to seduce her
with imaginations of future beauty.

KATHARYN HOWD MACHAN

I WON'T WRITE A POEM TONIGHT

It's too hot
to lament, to complain, to put
the world to rights with words:

swans protesting
at being forced to winter,
a man's pure body

needing wildest sex.
Past middle age I've read
the classics, gold

to touch and tongue and mind,
and in my bed I have
a husband

with a tattoo of Pan
on his arm. Let
me wear soft blue

from breast to thigh,
spring's perfume sprayed
on secret skin. Death

looks at me and laughs
again. I'm his. My breath
has rhymed, not rhymed, alone

finding a life few myths
have dared. My gravestone
will be bright and heavy:

a gaudy necklace at a sidewalk
sale, a silenced daughter's
cry to be loved.

HOW NOT TO WRITE A POEM

Allow a loved one's illness
to get in the way of your pen
or keyboard or stick in the sand
or even the voice that calls in
your dreams bellowing villanelles.
Say it's your daughter. Say she's

twenty-two and addicted to dope
so you can't do a god-blessed
thing because she's a legal adult.
Go to Al-Anon, live the Twelve Steps,
whittle your guilt to a small
tight splinter and flick it into

hot flames. The places where you keep
your stanzas will disappear in dust.
Vaguely you'll remember needing
enjambment, metaphors, rhyme—
but they're all forgotten now.
You just don't have the time.

DEBORAH PRATT CURTISS

GOING NUDE

I doubt that I came into this world a brat, but I became one at a young age. Some people opine that we are born with a particular temperament; others declare personality is acquired. For me, it's a complex concoction of nature-nurture plus experience that has shaped who I was, and whom I have become.

"Don't ever try to feed this baby on a schedule. She'll never let you get away with it," the nurse advised my mother upon leaving the hospital with me as a newborn. As a child, when my mother told me, "There are some things boys can do that girls can't," I grew defiant, feisty, questioned authority, back-sassed and otherwise challenged, or resented, anyone who tried to lord it over me.

And try they did. For much of my life I have encountered people, mostly males, who have attempted to diminish me, make me smaller than I am. Now, looking down the slope to my not-so-far-away but not imminent demise, some acquaintances valorize my intelligence and accomplishments. My reality resides suspended in the murky abyss between insignificance and glory.

As I eke out truth, I wonder what I would have become if my intelligence had been nurtured from the beginning instead of being reared to fulfill traditional female functions. When I was a teenager in the 1950s, my father advised, "Every great man has a woman behind him, and that's your ideal role . . . but get a teaching certificate, just in case."

In case of what, that I'd fail to land a husband? That if I succeeded in that, but he died or left me, I could support myself? I wasn't interested in becoming a schoolteacher. I yearned for something more challenging, something that would continue to provoke me throughout my life to become stronger and better than I was the day before. So I resisted. Replete with resentment, I fought back, but for just what, I was unable to discern as my ignorance of other options kept getting in my way. I therefore followed my mother's example, and studied art and philosophy so I could at least be an educated wife and mother.

Through six years of college and art school to a BFA in painting, I had only male professors, not a single woman. Nor did I know any woman who might provide an example of being more than a housewife or teacher, nurse or secretary. One art school critic averred that I was "the best painter in the school." Another responded to my paintings as, " . . . decorative and ridiculous. Stop wasting your [and my] time." Taking this latter one seriously, as more probable than becoming a significant artist, I gave up painting and worked in city planning and urban redevelopment for four years. Other than secretaries (one assigned to me), there was only one other woman, also a junior administrator, both of us paid less than the men in the same position. Without knowing or encountering any woman who exemplified what it was that I yearned to be and do, I fell back on what I did know. By age twenty-eight, in direct and unequivocal denial of my questing nature, I had become a college faculty wife, housewife, and mother of two. Period.

Like an unbroken filly, I chafed and thrashed in multiple directions to assert my worth: painted bold abstractions, aggressively debated political science professors living in the same faculty warren, and sang semi-professionally with Medieval and Renaissance music groups with my then husband, a mathematician/lutenist.

Years earlier, at my first life-drawing class in art school, I was startled when a graduate student I knew through music, doffed her robe, stepped up on the model stand and stood naked in her generous, Rubenesque beauty. I immediately sensed I would never tire of studying the human form. Twelve years later, the day that my son joined his older sister in nursery school three mornings a week, I hired a student from the college to model for me so I could draw and paint what I loved. As nature's most complex, magnificent, and challenging form, to me the nude figure in art is a metaphor for humanness, humanity, and western art itself. It's comforting to know that I'm not alone in esteeming it so. Michael Taylor in *Rembrandt's Nose* writes, "Rembrandt has given us a mythological equivalent of the relationship between the artist and the [nude] model or, to put in more general terms, between the artist and the world."

Evidently, in my small world at the time, I was alone with this point of view. In my husband's eyes, and anyone else's of my acquaintance, it seemed that a nude is simply a nude—no place for metaphor—and my ambitions were misguided. Others perceived my art and music as "nice hobbies," never meant to be taken seriously, for my basic task was to serve and care for my husband, children, and home.

One evening at dinner, having endured years of dismissive criticism, I was provoked by my husband's comment, "You can't even get dinner on the table in forty minutes," to snap. I threw my dinner against the wall, stood up, screamed and stamped my feet in rage. In those moments, I lost control, pride, care, and propriety. Several hours later as I recovered my composure, I realized that it was the most authentic thing I had done in a very long time— perhaps ever.

Having recognized the sham I had been living, a year and a half later, in 1972 when my children were seven and nine years old, like Ibsen's Nora, I left my family. I moved just eleven miles away, near enough to share custody and care of my children, but into the city where I could thrive among cultural stimulants and interactions with kindred spirits. I set up my studio in the main room of my apartment, found a gallery to exhibit my work, and got a job at Philadelphia Museum of Art teaching basic drawing initially, and later figure drawing and advanced painting as well.

My role in life transformed from being an auxiliary, to the pathfinder in my own universe—and the sole, scant breadwinner as I strove to make ends meet with part-time teaching and freelance singing. "Elegant poverty" is what my daughter dubbed my lifestyle when, as a teenager, she chose to live with me full-time, my son having made that choice a year earlier. After requesting child-support, to no avail, I had to sue their father for $40 per week. So we three struggled, but our life was authentic. *I* was authentic as I persevered in developing my art, and savored the vibrant, scintillating synergy between artist and subject.

Speaking of an artist's subject, when a model comes to my studio, I feel the weight of centuries of tradition. But it's a tradition built upon "the male gaze," decried by my fellow feminists as too often lascivious and prurient. Tales of artist-model affairs are rife. By contrast, I wanted to offer a different perspective as a painter of the human figure, one that evokes a sense of inner reality, and alternate realities—potentials rather than facts. Thus, my intent is neither realism nor lust, but a more intuitive and meditative expression. To that end, I try to establish an empathy with my models in which she or he and I, at least temporarily, become one. As many of my models are dancers, I ask them to move slowly, accompanied by classical music, within a small perimeter until I see a pose with which I relate. The poses I prefer tend to be complex, often foreshortened; views that we seldom experience, or get to contemplate in real life.

Guided by a questing eye, my exploring pencil wanders into an uncharted land, as it sings the melody of a model's body. It senses the lines of force that lie deep within every section of the human form. It follows contours that are never regular, but ever changing, point-by-point along the outline of an arm or breast. Each hand and foot demands as much time to draw as the torso, each feature of the face as much time as a hand. Thus the rhythm changes as I gradually and attentively examine every facet, compose and recompose a symphony with multiple key signatures and rhythms that every human being represents.

When I then create a painting from my drawings, I enter another world, one that is solely mine, over which I have total dominion. I am the investigator, the bumbler, the creator, and hearken to no one but myself. Working intuitively, I simultaneously strive to make something new, to look at something differently and thereby entice others to shift perspective. I rearrange both aspects and ideas to improve, to transform, to try out a variety of possibilities. I wander and probe mysterious realms, and revel in the process of discovering where my creative acts will lead.

My paintings and I dialogue: they speak to me, tell me what needs strengthening, what to soften, to brighten, to articulate more clearly. I eye-listen, eye-consider, I ruminate, and when I eye truth, I yield to its power and comply. By the time I complete a painting, we've sung and danced, we've made love, we've become one. And then I send it off, into the unbound world to fend for itself.

I am part of the outer world, too. As my life progressed, and my art accumulated and was exhibited, it became clear to me that, however much respect my paintings garnered, they would not bring me fame or fortune. During the 1980s, millions of square feet of vacant wall space became available in new office buildings, hotels, hospitals, museums and other public structures. Galleries bloomed, the art market heated up exponentially, and neither my art nor I was part of it. I found it ironic, and continue to do so, that television, movies, advertisements, and entertainment may be rife with nudity and sexuality, but an art nude in a public place other than a museum, is considered indecent, or anticipated as potentially offensive to clients and customers.

Stubbornly, I stuck to my passionate love of the nude, evolving in my approach from flat shapes, to a celebration of contours (outlines) limning otherwise flatly painted figures, to depicting one "scape"—imaginary or landscape—within a body, another outside of it, and eventually to celebrating light and shadow—how shadows can both reveal and conceal form. In this latest approach, my love of adventure was expressed by using a watercolor technique with thinned acrylic paints, staining into raw (unprimed) canvas in which there is no opportunity to correct mistakes. I came to quip, "If necessity is the mother of invention, mistake is surely the father." Feeding my need to fulfill my own potential, my paintings evolved as well: increased in quality, complexity, sophistication, and even size. Many were too large for most homes, which seemed the sole venue outside of museums for paintings of the nude figure.

Some of my figure paintings have never been exhibited in any public space, not even a gallery. Gallery directors who visited my studio wondered whether I could paint something else. Their questions and comments insinuated that I had a fixation that others simply didn't share.

During periods when insufficient income meant no pay for models, I kept my eye-mind-hand coordination sharp by drawing botanical forms—plants, flowers, trees—subjects that were plentiful and readily available anywhere. I filed these eye-calisthenic artifacts away, and gave them no other thought until a gallery director saw some lying about my studio. He offered me a solo show of paintings that were based on, or inspired by, these elegant line drawings. I complied in 1990.

As I was writing this essay, I held an exhibit of the last of these botanical paintings—along with some of the drawings, and subsequent prints and collages—still in my possession. The four-hour show celebrated Spring, Earth Day, and Arbor Day, 2014, and was held in the studio and home of my dreams where I have lived since 1992. At the time I moved into this artists' cooperative, as a co-founder, I lacked a teaching job and worked full-time in a large architecture firm as a writer/editor. Coincidentally, the firm gave me my first solo show in Philadelphia, in 1972, just before I moved into the city. In 1993, knowing that I was a painter, its key designer asked me to commemorate one of his buildings for exhibit in the firm's lobby. I placed a sky-scape within the high-rise building's silhouette, and the surface colors and textures of the building in the place of the sky. It remained on view for three years, and resulted in an invitation to join Tabula Rasa, an international, multi-cultural exhibiting group composed of artists who, like myself, earned their livings in the design professions. As I responded to Tabula Rasa exhibition themes, which we chose through a consensual process, I was weaned from the nude as my primary subject. To minimize withdrawal symptoms, I traveled to Prague for inspiration and, while drawing its architecture, incorporated nude figurative sculptures that adorn many of its buildings.

In 1999—my children grown, married, and parents themselves—I married John, whom I effortlessly adored, and I knew he held me in high esteem. He and I vowed to encourage one another in following our own paths. While I continued to paint and evolve my vision, he became the artist he never previously dared to realize, and produced photographs and constructed wood and metal sculptures that garnered immediate recognition. By the end of 2003, continuing to live frugally, I had saved enough from working twelve years at the architectural firm and five years teaching up to six graduate seminars per year at the University of the Arts, to retire and devote myself, once again, to full-time painting.

A month later, we learned John had multiple health problems, including cancer. As we addressed his health needs, both of us continued to work in our studios. Unstuck from the human figure, I floundered with experiments and a variety of subjects, and it wasn't until 2008 that I found a sufficiently challenging theme: "Meditations on a Post-Human Earth." Inspired by overpopulation and the ravaging of our lonely planet, I developed the imagery from small collages I had been making while we addressed John's health issues. The collages include various papers, drawing elements, pressed orchids, and used contact lenses that I honor as coconspirators in my incisive visual perception. In a radical departure from my previous paintings, in which I considered composition as fundamental, I juxtaposed and superimposed three collages at random to achieve the imagery of the Meditation paintings. These paintings are highly contemplative in process, content, and affect.

Two years after beginning the Meditation paintings, my ability to concentrate evaporated when we learned John's cancer had metastasized. I was too distracted by his health challenges to trust what I would do in the studio, and stopped painting, devoted myself to his care and creative fulfillment, and made more small collages as opportunity permitted. John took his last photograph five days before, and worked in his sculpture studio three days prior to dying peacefully in his sleep, in our bed as I held his hand next to my heart, April 2011.

In the year following his death, as part of the daunting process of reclaiming and redefining my life as a single, I turned to and completed the remaining ten Meditation paintings: twenty-eight in all, one for each letter in the title phrase, Meditations on a Post-Human Earth. And I have not painted since. To my astonishment, writing has taken painting's place. Having published two art-related books and uncounted informational and scholarly articles and chapters in my past life, my desire to learn to write creatively came to dominate my present. I joined a writing group with an excellent coach and peers. I take courses and, for more than two years, have been writing a river.

Due to this new passion, I've neglected procuring opportunities for the Meditation paintings to be exhibited. I want them to be shown together, for them to create a meditative environment and atmosphere. Painted on linen, cotton, and silk canvases, each has four sides of unequal lengths, and lacks any specific orientation, horizontal or vertical. My intention is that they emanate an evanescent instability, like shards of the fragmented and complex lives most of us live at this point in time. They are to be hung in any direction, order, or configuration that fits the space in which they appear. As such, I deliberately invite curatorial intervention and invention. My hope is that I will find curators who, as artists in one form or another themselves, will savor such a challenge and opportunity.

Dedicated to Mary Stieglitz, PhD
Colleague, cherished friend, and inspiration.

MARY KAY RUMMEL

FRAGMENTS

Violet-haired Sappho
praised purple hyacinths
crushed beneath the sandaled feet
of passing soldiers.
Praised amethyst
last color before dark.

Praised women who lie down
in wild thyme, purple crocus,
who wind sprigs into unbound hair,
who speak dill and quince-apple
shaking pollen into shapely ears.

Ancients said the head of Orpheus
washed up with bladder verach
on her island, still singing.

They called her tenth muse,
genius deformed by gender.
Called her harlot, burned
her poems.

She escaped the flames
in fragments we translate,
ashes we rearrange.
Thousand-petaled, she is sifting
down to us.

PATRICIA BARONE

RISING AND FALLING

From the other end of the long table, Ann's oblong face, collapsed into wrinkles close up, was whole. White hands against black shirt, her cigarette's calligraphy, spirals of smoke on a peach horizon.

Sarah, Alice's daughter, walked into the frame. Alice put her camera down. Sarah slid Ann's dessert plate onto the tray she held—were they arguing?

No wonder—taking unfinished teiglach out from under people's forks!

Alice hated the end of her backyard parties—the first fork across the middle of a dessert plate, the first hand over a coffee cup, the way people sat back and looked past each other.

Grandma Ann returned to her conversation, ignoring Sarah, then she patted the pocket where she kept her writing notebook and stood up.

So did a few others. The damage was done. Now Alice couldn't wait for everyone to go.

⋊⋉⋊⋉

She would have liked to settle back among the fragments of their meal, look at the stars coming out, and have a good gossip with Danny. But she had to find Sarah.

Loading the dishwasher, Sarah didn't turn around when Alice said, "I'm sorry for snapping at you, Sweetie. Thanks for helping."

When Sarah didn't say anything, Alice got ticked—"*Why* did you argue with Grandma?!"

"Grandma was a show off, asking me personal questions in front of people. Usually I avoid her when she's like that. So do you!"

"That's complicated. You don't carry the old history. I do. You start fresh. She admires you."

Sarah made a face. "I used to think I was her favorite, but if she admires me, she has a funny way of showing it. She made me move so Sister Jean could sit next to her."

Alice chuckled, and Sarah said, "Don't make fun of me!" Rage in her eyes.

"I wasn't laughing at you, just the situation." A tentative arm around her shoulder, but Sarah shook her off, and the willow-pattern cream pitcher she held fell into the sink. They watched the spout break off the bowl.

"No big deal," Alice said, but Sarah was already up the stairs. A door slammed.

☒☒☒

"It gets so chilly now once the sun goes down. Come in for just a few minutes. I'll fix us a hot spiced cider," Ann said. The invitation echoed plaintively in her own ears. Angry at herself, Ann turned away from Jean and fumbled with her key ring. Don't let me age before Jean does! She leaned forward, putting all her weight, such as it was, on the oak, to bring the warped wood into alignment, and the bolt rasped back. "But maybe you'd rather not. You have work tomorrow."

"Hot cider would be nice," Jean said. "Let me do it."

Ann watched Jean walk away—out of her habit and swinging her trim hips. No nunny suits for her. Ann's eyes filled and she collapsed on a hard chair, a tear falling on her old, old hands.

From the pantry, Jean's voice was muffled, ". . . out of cinnamon sticks? No . . . " Jean backed in through the swinging kitchen door.

She ought to help, Ann thought, but couldn't stop staring at her feet, gray leather pumps.

Jean carried the tray with its steaming mugs into the living room and put it on a low table in front of the love seat facing the fireplace. "You look cold. I'll start a fire."

"Oh . . . yes. Yes." Maybe Jean would stay.

☒☒☒

Alice turned her back on the pots and pans. No way to recapture that respite she might have imagined—when her home deepened and grew still and people she loved came to play and no time passed at all.

She stood at the back door. The four o'clocks in the dusk were small jewel-colored circles. Some streaked in magenta and gold—an unlikely accident, her home-made hybrids. The plum had turned too soon—mottled

yellow leaves falling on the hostas.

The garden was like an elderly woman with abundant hair. On the day when every plant had stretched as far as it could grow, each began to thin. As soon as the Jerusalem artichokes finally opened their brief sunflowers, their leaves fell. The family will finally find things. Maybe the artichokes had taken her oldest son's baseball and her earring. Last summer several odd sandals and a spatula reappeared in the zucchini patch.

The children have been shedding since the day they came home from the hospital: plastic parts of trucks, archeological layers of Ranger Ricks, crayons, apple cores, rubber wheels. She shuts the drawer on jam-fingered marbles and odd buttons. Let them multiply in the dark.

Danny put his hands on her shoulders. "I know what you need." She leaned her head back against his yielding girth. So restful to be interpreted, his hands in a warm massage upon her neck. But it made her feel difficult. She wasn't sure herself how she felt. Unaccountably sad when she saw Naomi, her youngest, return to her grandmother's lap, so warm from playing tag that damp curls stuck to her cheeks. Alice had a fleeting image of herself at five, running around the periphery of the same garden, screaming with excitement. Families have little ghosts. No one ever grows up unless a procession of children are lost. Her own photographs knew. Captured as she went out the door the first day of her senior year, Sarah's face was tense. Alice could almost see the words, "Mom! I'll miss my ride!" Naomi gone half a day to kindergarten.

Danny pulled out a chair and rested his elbows on the table, slouching. "Well?"

"It's not Ann. I don't want the children to grow up."

Danny laughed. "Most women would be all tired out getting four children out the door with thirteen years still to go!"

Alice began digging jam from between the grooves of the table molding with a bread knife. His voice amused, knowing. He made it sound pointless— her feelings. All flattened out. She'd almost had something there. Like a rabbit on the edge of the lawn.

Ж Ж Ж

Ann made an effort, rising to her feet on one breath, and made it onto the love seat. Now here she was—almost catatonic. Was she getting strange? The cider slid down her throat without incident. Past what she imagined as a narrowing. So often she found it hard to breathe—as if through a pinch in her windpipe. She'd be driving the car and suddenly her ears would be warm, a little pulse would start half way down her neck, and she'd think—I'm going to choke! Then the feeling went away. Psychosomatic, or real? The thought was a clamp on her temple.

"Are you worried about something?" Jean asked.

Ann took a deep breath. "Oh, the U wants me out. The chairman said he notices the small press is much more appreciative of Midwestern talent these days. Translation—Why hasn't *The New Yorker* published my poems recently? He's been hinting about how, at my age, I can't be expected to carry more than two workshops. Any *more* than! I deserve to end my days as artist-in-residence—not a workhorse. He'd *like* me to retire.

"I'll enter your religious order and teach at your college. Seriously. I would've taken the veil years ago, but you gave yours up for permanents." She felt better already. Jean always did her good.

But Jean was looking at her with a very slow expression, half her face lost as a smile went from left to right and disappeared. Fog around her ear.

Maybe still a little tipsy from Alice's garden party. Maybe cataracts. She pressed the heel of her palms into her eyes and, when she raised her head, Jean looked just the same as usual: broad-faced and—Jean loved her.

"Are you feeling sick?" Jean's blue eyes grew bigger in circles of light from the fire, her temples scalloped by the edge of her thick lenses. "Should I call the doctor?"

Ann leaned back into cushions. Jean's face receded, but she kept it in focus all the way back to the small easy chair next to the Dutch-tiled hearth. The room settled into minute order. Safe. She took a sip of her cider. "I felt a little dizzy or something, just a second. Must be tired, I'm all right now." Never better. A contained fire burnished the brass lampshade. Another lapped in her grandmother's mirror over the carved table. Time to take it easy, live in one small room.

After Jean left so slowly her voice lingered, Ann went to bed. A black shade fell, she slept.

)(○)(○)(

"I'm sorry I hurt your feelings," Alice said. "Don't mind me, I get goofy."

Sarah lay on top of her comforter in a bright pink chenille bathrobe, her red hair a formidable cloud behind her. A book was propped in front of the pillow she rested on, and she didn't look up. "And sorry for getting on your case about Grandma."

Sarah told her to forget it and Alice sat down next to her, resisting the impulse to pat her bottom. "It's just that I hate it when people rush through the good meal I've cooked for hours."

"Mom, forget the mosquitoes? And if you want people who appreciate your cooking, don't invite Grandma. All she does is smoke, drink, and talk. You only see what you want to see."

Maybe that was the problem. Everything in her life just happened—the way things did in dreams. She felt a hollowing in her stomach. Was that really the way Sarah saw her? A cotton candy sort of mother? Well, at least she wasn't the sort of mother with sharp edges. When you push away a mother with sharp edges, like Ann, you get hurt. With one hand, Alice cupped the springy mass of Sarah's hair, so like her own. She kissed her cheek.

Ӿ⊙Ӿ⊙Ӿ

Ann woke all at once, as if it were morning. Still dark. A hiss from the grate in the living room. She never went to bed before the fire was out. No more sleep till she checked it and peed. Where's Great Grandma's chamber pot? As she put her weight on her elbow and began to rise, a pain began in the back of her head and traveled to her temple, radiating down her arm and leg—stitching her body to the bedclothes. "No!" she said and fell—ripping a seam as she went.

Ӿ⊙Ӿ⊙Ӿ

Alice's thoughts jumbled, she couldn't fall asleep. All right, poor reception, you need fine tuning. She put her hand on Danny's thigh, but he only snorted with the beginning of a snore. Danny had a trick of easy sleep she envied. Night after night, there she was on the surface doing her survival float, and there he was down below—loose limbed, swimming deeper all night.

She slept and woke, it seemed, minutes later. The clock said 4 a.m. In her dream she'd been fishing, no pole, no line. She sat on the dock and all the fish swayed in the water below her, like sea anemones. Her garden. Then one bleeding fish broke the water, a large hook in its mouth.

Ӿ⊙Ӿ⊙Ӿ

Sister Jean felt the light in her bedroom like a presence even before she opened her eyes. Through the high transom, a winged shape flew to her cot and hovered. She threw back her covers—Jesus, Mary, Joseph!—and jumped up dressed in red. Too late to hide! But the winged thing rose—a crackle of veil in starched distress—and flew through the narrow window.

She turned over, groped for her glasses. Damn, must have kicked the cord out of the socket getting into bed last night. Still early by the light. She and Ann could breakfast together.

Last night's clothes tossed in an untidy heap on the chintz chaise lounge. She'd change her blouse to something cheerful. Not red.

When she came down, Sister Agnes was peering at the paper. How restful having a housemate who didn't like to talk in the morning. Would be quite a different story if she lived with Ann.

Outside, a soft September rain. The sort of morning for lingering over a second cup of coffee, but she had a nagging sense she'd forgotten something. About Ann . . .

⋊⋊⋊

She bent to pick the Tribune out of Ann's straggly shrubs. Heartburn rising in her throat, she hit the lion-head knocker, rat-a-tat. And leaned on the bell. Ann said its raucous peal would wake the dead. Hands and knees on the wet lawn, she pulled on bricks. The loose one—key!

Her fingers shaking, she turned it then rushed up stairs so fast she had a side stab.

Ann lay across her bed, her right leg straight, one satin slipper hanging from the tips of her toes, her left leg bent at the knee. Be alive! She put her ear on Ann's chest.

"A stroke," Jean told the voice on 911. "Yes, unconscious." She almost gave her own address, then, with great effort, slowly gave Ann's.

" . . . an ambulance on the way . . . .stay on line." The voice pressed down on Jean's strange calm. "Airway clear? Does she have a bluish color on lips, nose, or hands?"

"Is she breathing? Her chest goes in and out too slow. She's white, cold!"

"Take her pulse."

Ann's wrist felt clammy. Jean fumbled—all the arteries collapsed! Then she found it—a faint, unsteady beat on the edge of stop.

"Could you estimate what time the patient was stricken?"

How should *she* know? If she'd spent the night—she should have—she'd know.

"Time of the stroke?" the voice repeated and Jean filled with unreasonable anger.

"*I don't know*! Between 10:00 p.m. and 7:30 a.m."

)X(X(

Once the attendants placed Ann's stretcher on the narrow cot receiving it, attached her machines, and strapped her into place, a young medic gave Jean a hand up.

Inside, as the siren preceded them to the hospital, Jean stared at Ann's face—drawn down, distorted; an eyetooth snarling. Why couldn't they go faster!

"Don't worry," said a first responder. "She's not so bad." Jean filled with gratitude but she couldn't speak. How long had she been crying, the tears seeping out and running down?

)X(X(

Ann's pupils looked too wide for seeing.

"Moth—er!" Alice said, her breath in gasps.

Sarah took Alice's arm. "Calm down, Mom."

"Ann, you've had a stroke, you're in the hospital," Jean said.

"Who," Ann said, "Who!"

The nurse explained that sometimes stroke patients understood but words didn't come out right. "Do you know where you are? Nod your head if you do," she told Ann.

Ann moved her head to the side.

"*Mom,* it's Alice."

A drawn out, "Whooooo."

A doctor was saying her mother might not be severely aphasic, though the injury was primarily to the left brain.

"Her speech center—no! She has to write her poems." Jean reached back for a chair that wasn't there, but Alice caught her.

"Find meaning," Jean mumbled. "A grace she survived . . . maybe . . . "

"Remember that time at the zoo," Alice said, seeing herself at ten, chocolate ice cream on her sun dress and the gravel. Pleading with Ann sprawled on the bench. Mom laughing, licking her cookie cone then talking gibberish. "I was so *scared*. You came to take us home . . . "

"Yes, no . . . I took her to the hospital."

"Then Grandma was *alright*, Mom!" Sarah squeezed Alice's arm.

"That small stroke predicted this big one!" Jean's veiny hands gripped the side rail.

"Does she remember, think, feel?" Alice asked the nurse, who murmured, "Too early to tell."

"Trapped in her own body . . . " Sister Jean moaned, and Alice felt a clarifying stab of dread.

Ann heard voices but couldn't say, except "Who, who, whooooo!" then song came out—

"There was an old woman tossed up in a basket, oh! . . . seventeen times as high as the moon . . . "

"What did she say?" Sarah asked.

"Moon?" Alice whispered. "Moon."

"Listen!" Jean hissed.

Song out of this mouth! Ann put the hand that moved on her mouth— *wind!*

> *Trapped in her own body—no!*
> *But she sinks to the bottom of the sea.*
> *Their faces swim up from under water.*
> *No, they peer down on*
> *me, the mermaid with a seal's face,*
> *whiskered walrus.*
> *Voices echo on my eyes,*
> *familiar faraway voices—*

"It's us, Ann. Jean and Alice!"

"And Sarah!"

> *Their words come down on waves, my sonar,*
> *and bounce off me—I*
> *sing back whale songs*
> *from my rib cage cathedral.*

"There was an old woman tossed up in a basket seventeen times as high as the moon!

Old woman, old woman, old woman, said I.

Where are you going up so high?

To sweep the cobwebs out of the sky!

Shall I go with you?
Yes, by and by."
Yes, by and by!
"Down will come Baby, cradle and all . . . "
down to the bottom of the sea
where loving faces watch me drown
and I can't speak.

)X()X()X(

I really captured them, Alice decided, looking up at the wall in her home studio, all she had the energy to do. This short, fat woman in a Romanesque gray veil and flowing white gown was also Sister Jean—the way she looked when she rescued Ann and ten-year-old Alice from the zoo.

The framed print of Ann at work on Alice's wall was set off on either side by clumped branches—oval in mass, rising in the center, black at the roots, ascending dark red branches, silvering twigs that ended in an ingrown tangle.

The shape of the bramble bushes repeated the shape Ann's hair had then—curly, weighty, ending above her shoulders, her face a perfect oval on the mass of black.

The arrangement with Ann was the best Alice ever made, so she never changed it, and she looked at it again and again. Taken on the University of Minnesota campus, the photo showed Ann sitting on a low camp stool, leaning forward, elbows balanced on her knees as she gestured, her hands outstretched, cupped. The students were sprawled about on the grass under a large chestnut tree. Ann was talking about poetry and the candles of the tree were white as her face.

III
ARTISTIC PROCESS

DIANE GIARDI

IN THE STUDIO

Intent and accident
toy with each other,
sometimes keeping their distance-ice cold chill,
turn your back
they're flirting-hot and dangerous.
This week I'm convinced they're good for each other,
sobering, balancing, vital truth of transience.
Last week I cried I would forever keep them apart.
Impossible fancy.
One and the same,
they are married.
Water and sand——sometimes flowing,
tonight damned.
By morning a pool forms.
A small fish is swimming.

JO GOING

LANDSCAPE PAINTING WITH MITTENS ON

I could freeze to death,
found years later,
a solid ice block——
painter, paint, and paper.

The paint tubes crack,
the water freezes,
and mittened hands
are a tundra clown act.

The good part—
you can't dawdle for hours,
slouched over the small self,
scratching, muddletating,

for the brush must
cross ten thousand miles
in one sure stroke . . .
or the paper frosts.

This far North,
where land is the measure
of what to grow into,
landscape painting

with mittens on,
an acquired technique
not taught in art school,
is one's own measure.

MARY KAY RUMMEL

HAIKU LADDER

"Haiku saves lives." Sonia Sanchez

It gets inside you
deep like the blues, and deeper,
a river rising.

I was a young nun.
My mind prowled through syllables
beast hungry for words.

I could buy one book.
My twentieth year Basho
fell like a ripe plum

into my desperate hands.
His poems mirrored my mind.
Simply alive with them

I grew Haiku eyes.
The short lines slipped from my hand
flew into the world.

May evening shower
petals from the wild rose bush
moon light on the ground.

My thrown rock, became
Basho's frog plopping lidless
into convent pond.

Rings of water churned
silver dancers leapt shoreward.
Inside and outside

green growing wood weeds
covered the eyes of the priests—
"Recall you are dust."

The winter white pine
gives ice a place to hang on.
So haiku saved me.

ROSEMARY VOLZ

PLUM

Sitting at Aunt Pauline's dinning room table
Eyeing the perfect purple plum in a crystal bowl,
I grab it and bite down into an imposter.
Mouth full of wax, my aunt laughing at me,
I squeeze back the tears and smile
But in my clumsy childish way
I wrap the moment in an oversized box
And in my time of moons and blood, I open it
And vow I will never deceive the senses.
I will be a daughter of flesh and juices,
Never poured batter-like into a mold
Never corseted and powdered into a
Comfortable and doughy acceptability.
I will rebel against plastic doilies,
Blue carnations and counterfeit desires.
I will live with a reckless honesty
I will demand a terrible freedom.

Years later at Aunt Pauline's funeral
She lay drained and polished to a synthetic sheen,
Lilac lipstick, lavender lace dress.
Deception was all around her rouged cheeks
And I remembered my vow
And how arrogant I was to defy the natural
Order of things.

LAURENCE SNYDAL

COOPERATION

> *"While you are reading, you are the book's book."*
> *Ralph Waldo Emerson*

Now I look at you between my words
And tell you what I think you want to know.
And you and I agree that these words go
Just where we think they should. They are like birds
In their coveys. When I call, you answer.
You read what I write. I must look to you
For recognition. You wait for my cue
To follow. Then I become the dancer
Who insists on following you. I lead
Your eye as you anticipate my rhyme
And so we find ourselves both trapped in time
And type and triteness. You know you don't need
Me for reassurance nor I you. Yet
I feel impelled to write these lines until
I tire of writing or your eyes grow still
And stubborn. And so I suppose we get
A feeling of communication here
And maybe something more. Why you persist
In reading this is something that I missed.
But missing that, I have to make it clear
That my reflections mirror yours. No doubt
I need you looking in as I look out.

STRUCTURE

Function follows form. As the course is set
So it is run. The lime lines laid with post
And string out on the lawn define what's closed
To grass and green and open to instead.
Covers label books. Words are bound to get
More binding, pressed and printed. The almost
Of all we know as process is proposed
As pattern, falls on preset paths. Ahead,
Behind, is synapse, circuit. As I'm tracked,
I track myself and as I am, I act.

WIND CHILL FACTOR

We carry our own atmosphere, a thin
Slick of warmth and wet, aura, psychic sweat,
Insulation for an innocent skin,
Protective cover's cover. We forget
It's there until a chilly bit of breeze
Whisks it away. It's then we feel the true
Ambient temperature. It's then we freeze,
Open to weather and its residue.

The same glaze surrounds my cherished thinking,
Resisting alteration till a gust
Of speculate sets my mind's eye winking,
Blinking away the chimera of trust.
Intuition guides the active actor.
Insight is the artist's wind chill factor.

JOEL WACHMAN

THE OWNERSHIP OF DESIRE

Marta had no trouble keeping herself occupied while Luis was away seeing clients in the city. She was an accomplished artist, having sold several paintings to galleries in the city. She worked in oils that she mixed herself to make colors that were so intense that they shocked the eye. She worked on enormous canvases that she constructed inside the bungalow and had to slide edgewise through the doors. She painted insects, small birds, delicate flowers, all manner of diminutive thing magnified to several hundred its normal size. The fluttering of butterfly wings; the glistening of a spider's ovipositor; the striations on the leaf of a buttercup.

When the weather was warm Marta liked to work with the windows open, wearing only a running bra and a pair of Luis's boxer shorts. In the winter she would leave the windows open but put a wool cap on her head. She worked with the radio tuned to good rock stations and set to maximum volume. She would hold her long brush in her hand like a conductor's baton, sweeping it from palette to canvas and back again. After a few hours of this her body would be covered with paint. Leaving the radio on and the windows open, she would shower and sit with her back to her most recent piece and drink a large mug of coffee.

It was during one of these moments that she saw the scooter pull up the driveway. If the music had been off, Marta would have heard the telltale crunch of tire on gravel, perhaps also the whine of the Vespa's cylinders. But it was the motion through the window that caught her attention.

The scooter came to a stop just in front of the door. The man who dismounted was tall and muscular, with an angular face and short hair. He wore a white sleeveless T-shirt and shorts, heavy boots and thick socks. Under his arm he carried a black artist's portfolio. It would not have fit on the back of the scooter, so Marta concluded he must have been driving one-handed. The man leaned the scooter on its kickstand and headed along the gravel path towards Luis's office at the back of the house. This man must be a patient of

Luis, and thinking kindly that he must have confused his appointment time (though not all of Luis's patients were disturbed, the majority of them were so preoccupied with their troubles that they often had difficulty managing ordinary tasks like keeping appointments) Marta turned off the radio, put on a T-shirt, shorts and sandals, and went out to intercept him.

She saw him try the locked door. He seemed agitated and he jiggled the handle severely, even thought it was immediately obvious that there was nobody on the other side. When she came within ten feet of the man, he turned and saw her and his face lit up hopefully.

"He's not here," she said.

"When will he be back?"

"He's seeing patients in the city today. Do you normally see him here?"

The man gripped the artist's portfolio tightly in front of his chest. He looked down at it, then at her. "It's important," he said. "I'll wait."

Marta repeated, "He's working in the city. "Do you know where the office is, on Saint James Street?"

The man shifted his weight, looked at the locked studio door. Then at his scooter. Then at Marta.

"I'll call ahead for you, if it will help," Marta offered.

"Yes." The man said. Then, "But I don't know where the office is. You'll have to tell me that, too."

Marta turned to go back into the house for the phone. The man called after her, "Tell him it's . . . tell him it's Henri."

Luis's assistant answered the phone. Luis was in with a patient. Could she take a message? Marta told her about the man. There was a pause while the assistant weighed the urgency of Henri's particular case against the prudence of interrupting Luis in the middle of a session. Very soon Marta heard the telltale click of the call being transferred directly to the office phone, then Luis's voice.

"Hello, dear."

"Darling, a man named Henri is here. He seems agitated. He says it's urgent and needs to see you. Shall I send him over?"

"Yes. Yes, indeed. Send him over immediately."

"All right, see you—"

"Marta, dear, don't—"

There was a pause. A tremble in his voice. A subtle letting-go of what she liked to call his office voice and a lapse into his home voice. She could tell, in that tenth of a second, that he was looking for a way to say be careful.

"I'll send him right there," she said.

"Good. I'll see you tonight."

The phone went silent.

Outside, the man was pacing nervously around the scooter, his work boots kicking up dust in the gravel. He was clutching the portfolio and his face was twitching enough that Marta could have been forgiven for thinking he was mumbling. Marta thought he looked like the most lonely person ever born.

"Luis will see you in the city as soon as you can get there," she said.

Henri kicked the ground in frustration. A short growl escaped his throat. He looked up at Marta, dejected. "I don't know where the office is. I only see him here, and today isn't my day."

"Oh, well I can tell you how—"

"Take me there."

Marta searched for a kind way to refuse. Here was a frustrated man with psychological difficulties, asking her to mount a scooter with him and direct him six miles into the city. He seemed healthy, attractive, and strong. She found herself giving a watered-down excuse.

"I'm sorry. I couldn't possibly go. I'm working and I can't leave right now."

Henri saw right through her. "Look, if I have to find the place myself it could take hours. If you take me we can be there in ten minutes. Once we get there you can take the scooter back to the house. I'll come for it tomorrow. Your work can wait. I can't." He mounted the scooter and started the engine.

Marta saw a flicker of self-satisfaction in the man's eyes that to her surprise she found charming. If she went she would be helping Luis help this man, and that possibility felt good to her. She wondered what it was he needed to see Luis about. Did he have some sort of mental illness? Depression or schizophrenia maybe? Perhaps it was something as simple as girl trouble or a persistent inferiority complex that forced him to develop that rough exterior. It is impossible to tell whether a person sees a psychiatrist to exorcise demons or to work through minor annoyances. We could all use someone to talk to. She had finished her work for the day. She had the rest of the morning and all of the afternoon yawned in front of her. (If she went on the scooter with him she would have to put her arms around his body to hold on. She would be compelled to put her face near to his to shout out directions.) If she stayed at home she would clean up her paints, eat an early lunch, perhaps go for a walk. If she went with Henri, she might eat lunch in the city. Go to a bookshop. Visit the art store (hadn't she been running low on cadmium red?) But Luis's unspoken warning worried her. Whatever the reason, there was something about Henri to be wary of. Marta took a step towards the scooter.

"I'll give you very careful instructions and a map. It's not that hard to find, and if you run into trouble just ask anyone where Saint James Street is."

Henri did not try to argue with her this time. He held out his hand towards her. A moment of silence passed between them. Then two. Marta threw her leg over the seat of the scooter and put her hands on Henri's body to balance herself.

"Quickly," she said.

✗✗✗

Henri navigated the dirt road with one hand on the steering column and the other holding the portfolio. The Vespa was old—Henri had acquired it second hand from a friend who got tired of being hot or cold or rained upon, saying it was no better than being a pedestrian—the suspension had long ago worn out and he could feel every stone and minor ditch. It was difficult to maintain his balance, especially with the woman behind him changing the distribution of weight. Above all he was surprised at how much one extra person slowed the scooter so it whined and complained and barely broke fifty kilometers an hour. In a few moments they met the paved road with a hip-breaking bump and the scooter wound up to forty. Still, when it was just him the old Vespa could manage eighty, depending on the weather, and watching the cars speed past Henri felt a quick twinge of regret that he had taken her with him. She was slowing down the scooter and right now the most important thing was to get into that armchair, and say what he was aching to say. That was his only relief. Perhaps he should have taken the map, instead. But, no, the woman would take him directly to Luis's office (she probably went there nine times a week) and soon he would be seated in front of Luis talking, just talking, and Luis would say something that would cool the fire in his veins.

When they entered the city limits the traffic began to thicken. Cars roared around them, coming within inches of the scooter, then slowing in front of them forcing Henri to brake or swerve. Henri maneuvered deftly among them, accelerating wherever there was an opening, slowing and turning wherever there was danger.

)X()X()X(

Marta gripped Henri's torso for balance and she could feel the muscles tightening and relaxing as he drove. She tried not to grip too hard, not to make him feel she was *touching* him. If it were possible to hold a person with your hands and yet not have any physical contact, that is what Marta wanted to achieve. Henri took the exit that Marta indicated. At the bottom of the ramp they came up short next to an anonymous white panel van—one of those vans that roams the city by the hundreds without signage, the opaque windows hiding whatever shady activity is carried on inside. Marta told Henri to turn right when the light changed. The van was in the left lane and she assumed that it would turn left. Instead, the van turned right with the Vespa and soon was taking up too much room on the new road, squeezing them into the curb. The driver of the van was oblivious to the scooter (as well as the signs and lights that are intended to impose order on the chaotic streets) and without signaling or slowing turned right again at the next block. Henri squeezed the brake hard and leaned to the right to avoid getting hit. Marta's foot swung against the curb and she felt the skin on her ankle rub against the concrete. It surprised her. She had forgotten that she was wearing sandals. She looked down and saw one of the straps was broken and covered in blood.

"Are you okay?" Henri asked over his shoulder.

She could tell him the truth—that she was bleeding and in a little pain—but to what end? Would the man who was in a panic to get to Saint James Street stop on President Kennedy Boulevard to attend to her wounds? Besides, it was highly unlikely that Henri would have a first-aid kit in the tiny boot of the Vespa. She could hold out until they got to the office, then she would wash her ankle and put a plaster on it and all would be fine except for the regret of losing one of her favored sandals. Wounds like this always look worse when they are dirty and bleeding. The laceration itself was probably no larger than a coin. So Marta replied, "I'm fine." She didn't expect Henri to look behind him and see her bloody shoe.

"No you're not," he said over the traffic noise. At the next intersection, instead of turning left as she told him, he turned right and brought the scooter to a stop in an alley between two imposing stone buildings. They parked in front of a half-open door through which Marta could see the metal surfaces of a restaurant kitchen. Warm air drifted from the door carrying the smells of fried peppers and fish.

He bent down to take a closer look at her ankle, still clutching the artist's portfolio to his chest. Then, slowly and ever so gently, Henri touched Marta's foot just near the base of the second metatarsus, and then with his thumb and middle finger applied gentle pressure to the fibula. "Does that hurt?" he asked, not looking at her.

"No," she replied.

"It's not broken, then. I'll be right back." Henri rose and walked through the open door.

She waited, still and confused, breathing shallowly, eyes sweeping about the alley, for a period that seemed longer than just a few moments, until Henri emerged with bandages and alcohol swabs in his hands, and his ever-present artist's portfolio clutched to his chest under his elbow.

❌❌❌

Henri's knees cracked as he crouched down to attend to her wound. Her foot was long and delicate and despite the blood and the broken shoe—or perhaps just because of those things—it seemed quite beautiful. It had been a very long time since he had seen any part of a woman so close. When he had touched her foot earlier he remembered how a person could feel warm and harmless. Henri hesitated for a moment when he realized he could not bandage her foot while he was holding the portfolio. He closed his eyes for a brief instant. The panic was still there, only it had abated just enough to be perceptibly more bearable, enough to allow him to let go of the portfolio and lean it against the scooter. As he did so he felt the coolness of the sweat evaporating from under his arm where the portfolio had been, and he felt the freedom of moving his arms again without holding that thing. Nevertheless, with the portfolio out of his grasp (though still only inches from his body) he had to force himself not to rush through the next few moments while he was bandaging her foot. Gingerly, he undid the remains of the strap and removed Marta's sandal. He handed it up to her and she took it and for an instant Marta's hand and Henri's hand were touching the sandal simultaneously. Marta smiled gratefully and something else familiar rose up in Henri and he had to push it down, down, and finally look away.

❌❌❌

When Henri had finished he picked up the portfolio and stepped over the seat, ready to move on. The bandage felt snug and comforting to Marta. It took the edge off the sting. They had not said anything to each other since he went in to get the dressing, and Marta was full of questions.

"What is this place?"

"I work here," he said. He put his hand on the starter button but did not press it. It was difficult to hear what he said next, owing to the fact that he was facing away from her and also because he said it quietly, almost shamefully, "It's called Chez Henri."

Reaching over his shoulder, Marta touched the portfolio with one finger, not establishing enough contact with it to be threatening, just enough to indicate what she was talking about when she said into his ear, "I can hold that for you."

"No." Henri switched the portfolio to the other side of his body. Then, "Don't touch it. Don't *ever* touch it." He gave the accelerator a good twist and Marta almost fell off of the bike as they turned around in the alley and headed back into the city.

As it turned out, Luis's office was not far from Chez Henri. It was simply a matter of turning on to the avenue nearest the restaurant, navigating about the piles of automobiles double- and triple-parked at the side of the road and the ones that slowed to turn on to the smaller streets; watching out for the pedestrians who, brazen in their knowledge that they had legal right-of-way, strolled unhurriedly from curb to curb; then making one's way a half mile northward to School Street, the geographic center of the University section. A few blocks onward, after the revival cinema with the words "Roc y Horror" permanently affixed to the marquee, it was a quick slip up Saint James Street to the 1960's era tower block where Luis had rented an office ever since he had earned his degree and entered private practice.

It is fair to say that both Marta and Henri were relieved to arrive at the office block. Marta led Henri across the vestibule and pressed the button for the elevator. They stood side by side, looking straight ahead at the seam where the two doors met as the elevator rose diligently to the fourteenth floor. Marta could hear Henri breathing next to her. His breaths came unevenly, two or three quick shallow ones followed by a deep one which he drew in quickly in a conscious effort to calm himself, then let out slowly through his nostrils. His exhalations were disturbed by tiny shudders that she was certain he tried to hide. It was the shudders that made her feel tender. She was tempted to speak, but everything that came to mind seemed trite or inappropriate.

✗✗✗

Henri knew he only had moments to explain. He hadn't intended to find himself so physically close to her, in the alley behind the restaurant and now, here, in the confines of the elevator where he could smell her skin. Rosewater, acrylic paint, female sweat, laundry detergent, turpentine. Every molecule that entered him made his own skin grow hotter. Should he tell her why he needed to come? Don't be naive. She's the doctor's wife or girlfriend so of course she already knows about him. He probably tells her everything about his patients. Never using names, of course, but referring to them by syndrome. The one with the tic, the lonely one, the one who is afraid of heights, the retarded one, the divorcee, the one with the portfolio . . . came to see me today. Of course she seems like an intelligent woman who would have put two and two together already. But should he explain *why*. To him there was a reason, a story behind it. In these few moments he could explain how a certain child found himself in extraordinary circumstances, and how difficult it has become as an adult just to *cope*. Such a tall, well-built woman with just the right amount of flesh on her bones. Maybe if he told her she would let him touch her again, just a little. He could feel his grip on the portfolio tighten.

✗✗✗

The elevator opened directly into a well-appointed salon with paneled walls and oriental carpets, a bookcase in one corner and a healthy bouquet of chrysanthemums bursting out of a vase in the other. When Marta and Henri entered Marta stepped to the doorway of the assistant's office, put one hand on each side of the doorway and leaned in.

"Cara, is Luis available?"

Henri comforted himself by standing near the window and looking across the city. Just one more minute. Just seconds, he told himself. Hold on.

Finally Marta came out of the little office. "He's almost done with a patient," she said. "He'll see you in a few minutes."

"He's going to hate that you brought me here," Henri said into the window. "You should go."

"It's okay. I'll explain it to him."

"When you called him from your house did he tell you to stay away from me? Did he say I was dangerous?"

Marta laughed, a quick exhalation that sounded like "hah." She hadn't realized that Henri thought of himself that way. Now that he admitted it, she felt more vulnerable than at any time that morning. "No," she said, half truthfully. "He didn't say anything of the sort."

Henri turned and faced her, his eyes intense and angry. "You should have listened to him. You don't know me."

Marta whispered a reply, "I feel as if I do," but Henri had turned back towards the window. But her confidence in herself, in her ability to choose, her understanding of human nature and trust, this stack of beliefs that support the ego and super-ego had undergone a tectonic shift.

When Luis entered the room he saw Henri standing near the window gripping his portfolio and Marta sitting in a club chair rubbing at her bloody bandage. The mood in the room was dour and could have led a less intelligent and more jealous man than Luis to jump to irrational conclusions about how it got that way.

"Henri," he said. "I'm glad you decided to come see me." He motioned towards his office. "Please go in and sit down. I'll be with you in an instant."

Henri strode directly into the sanctum and closed the door without looking back at Marta, exiting her life as suddenly as he had entered it. Marta felt something tighten inside her. Luis put his hand on her shoulder then crouched down to look at her foot.

"Are you all right?"

"I'm fine," Marta replied. "We were on Henri's scooter. There was this moron driver of a van—Henri fixed it up."

Luis stood and looked down at her in the chair. "I told you not to, Marta."

"Yes, but he seemed so desperate."

"He is." Luis said. He squeezed her hand, then rose and took a step towards his office. "Come back in an hour. We need to talk."

Marta sat by herself in the salon for several minutes before leaving. She wished she could hear what Henri and Luis were saying. Wished for even a single word to slip under the door, cross the room, enlighten her. But the door was carefully designed and expertly installed and the only sound Marta could hear was the whisper of the air-conditioning.

She descended to the entrance level and stepped back into the city. The streets were full of the harshness of the sun and the clamoring of automobiles and crowds. Marta passed a bistro where she sometimes bought lunch, but she did not feel like eating. Instead, she walked across the boulevard and bought some paint at the art supply store, then she sat on a bench under a chestnut tree and watched as the city's afternoon played itself out.

When she returned the scooter was gone. Upstairs, Luis's door was open and he was sitting behind his desk. Marta went into the office and Luis came out from behind the desk and they embraced. Hot and tired from the city, Marta flopped down in the easy chair that patients used. By habit, Luis sat across from her.

"What made you go with him?" Luis demanded. "Even after I warned you?"

"He seemed—I don't know—like he needed someone."

"Marta," Luis started, "it isn't always possible to tell when someone is sick. People are not always what they seem."

"Henri said that, too."

"Yes, he knows he's sick. He is very disturbed and can be a threat to himself and to others." Luis paused. "Marta," he said. "You want to know what was inside that portfolio?"

"More than anything."

Marta had imagined a hundred things inside that portfolio. Drawings. A self-portrait, maybe. Some important papers related to Henri's past.

"It's a sixteen-inch butcher's knife. The kind one uses to slaughter animals. In Henri's kitchen it is simply a tool, but he is afraid he will use it on a person some day. He has a strong desire to use it on a person. Only the good and rational part of him—a part that gets weak sometimes—keeps him from doing so. So you can see he's constantly struggling with a terrible conflict. He needs to take his medication and come to his sessions regularly. But he is not someone you'd want to have as a friend. Or be close to in any way."

The shock of it brought her to tears. She began to cry outright, the pain and wetness wrung out of her in deep heaving sobs and, still not understanding where it was coming from, and quite involuntarily, she cupped her hands to her face and let out a high-pitched wail.

When she looked up Luis was standing beside her, his hands on her shoulders, his head bowed down so he could kiss her eyebrows, her forehead, her hair. He knew there was nothing to be said, not because he was a professional but because he understood her grief had its source in the deep and intimate failure to own one's desires, and instead to be owned by them.

After she had finished crying and after they held each other for another minute, Luis stood and returned to his desk.

"I have two more clients coming this afternoon. But I can bring my paperwork home and we can have an early dinner tonight. Will you be all right taking the bus?"

She nodded and managed a weak smile. She stood and left by the private exit, for there was a person waiting in the salon.

It took an hour for Marta to get home. The bus left her at the usual place, a half mile away from the house on a dusty road that needed paving. Marta was aware that her mind was absolutely quiet. She could think of nothing. She could not even think of something to think of. When she unlocked the door to the house she saw the painting she had been working on that morning before Henri arrived. Big hazy gelatinous bug eyes stared at her from the canvas, green and yellow. She had an urge to strike at it, to tear it apart, for it now seemed shallow and irrelevant.

She went into the kitchen and opened the knife drawer. She pulled out an eight-inch chef's knife and leaned against the counter. All of Luis's tools were of the highest quality, for he derived pleasure from organization and exactitude. She noticed how well balanced the knife was, how the shimmering blade tugged just slightly downwards. *I'm ready*, it seemed to whisper. *Just touch me to the surface of something that needs to be cut.* Marta closed her eyes and tried to imagine using the blade on a person, slicing into a living torso like a butcher cleaves a steak. She tried to imagine blood, but the closer the blade came to the imaginary body, the more ardent became her terror. She wanted to understand, but could not reach across that chasm. Luis was right about what it means to know someone. Until you look closely, so closely you can see all of the details, the connective tissue that holds one part to another, you remain strangers. Marta let the knife rest on the counter. The handle was damp with her sweat.

J. J. STEINFELD

PAST ARTISTRY

I can't describe how much I feel like changing my name. Not that I don't like Derrick Rellesmurn, but after what I've found out recently my name feels unreal, fabricated, worse than a lie. A Rellesmurn painting is worth a tidy little sum, just on the reputation of my name. A name I've been building artistically for thirty years, so changing it could plunge me back to square one. But everything seems wrong now and my name feels false, untrue. *Untrue.* What a smash-in-the-face revelation: for so long I had valued the truth, wrapped it around myself, considered it the basis of my art. I had become a worshipper of the truth. But my artistic pursuit of the truth sure hasn't prevented me from making money, lots of money. I don't feel any contradiction in that, but I don't want to get into any long discussion about art and money, the purity of creativity as opposed to the crassness of clawing after the bucks. I sold my first painting when I was fourteen and I've been making a good living from art since I was in my mid-twenties. I always seemed to have a way of attracting attention to my work, a strong hook: the artist who was nearly killed when he was fourteen by a suburban sniper who was never caught. All the elements for delectable myth and irrepressible legend, not to mention for the occasional horror story. I've had a full and fortunate creative life, a solid artistic career.

Then I turn to the sad-looking old man sitting on the bar stool next to me in an upscale air-conditioned lounge and he stares at me and I try without any luck to pull my eyes away from his gaze. If not here in this lounge, he would have found me somewhere else. He had tracked me down, this frail yet relentless hunter, me the human trophy less than an arm's reach away. Softly, without being threatening, he told me that he had known of my approximate location for about thirty years, but he had waited. Waited as he grew older and frailer. Waited until this wretchedly hot day in the middle of summer.

I had lived in order to paint, literally so, and what could be clearer, almost as if it were a shouted order from the Heavens. Paint, you worthless fool, the voice instructing me in no uncertain terms. How easily and precisely I can trace the start of my artistic career to a meaningless dot of history less than a minute in duration one late spring afternoon, when I was fourteen. If I had any talent then, I had a talent for concealing it. Antagonistic, purposeless, heading for a fall, that was a portrait of me at fourteen, willing myself into a life that would be short, undistinguished, and contemptible. I despised my middle-class surroundings—my parents, teachers, school, even the goddamn green lawns along which I walked each school day, when I bothered going to school. I despised everything I knew, even if my vision and experience were limited by suburbia and my youthful animosity. I learned to love art, and with it the world, at least the world as a place in which to be a painter. Even ugliness, when painted or depicted artistically, has a worth, I like to say, have been quoted as saying in more than one magazine article about my art and career.

I was walking home, full of anger and hostility, plotting something destructive. Then the first bullet struck me, in the right arm, and I fell to the ground. A second shot, striking the right shoulder, as I was lying on the sidewalk. I saw some sort of insect crawling nearby, picking up speed, starting to laugh. (I used that grotesque image in a painting several years later, just as I have used in my art nearly everything else connected to that time.) Next something tore into my left leg. I remember hearing a scream from someone a house or two away, like a sports announcer's loud declaration after an exciting play. I remember the silence that followed, a silence I couldn't measure, a silence during which I wondered if my arm and leg were still there. Then I saw blood. On my shirt and on my pants and on the sidewalk. Three more insects, carefully avoiding the river of blood. (Another future painting.) Soon after there was a neighbor's dog investigating my body, sniffing at my agony, as if the dog wanted to retrieve me. I saw the tires of an ambulance—my perspective was little better than the insects I was observing—and heard the commotion of the suburban afternoon routine being broken, then I didn't see or hear anything.

I have a larger than life-size painting—done when I was around thirty—of myself at fourteen waking in the hospital room, my parents standing over me, as close as I get to the surreal, the colors and shapes defiant. When it was actually happening, for an instant I thought I was home in my bedroom, the walls scarred with graffiti, and had a fear that my parents had found my stash of dope and were going to punish me. But their faces were overflowing with concern. Later two police officers arrived to question me. (Painting of them, too.) I was walking home from school, not doing anything wrong, I answered. Yes, I went to my fucking school that day, even though I had contemplated playing hooky. The little punk should have skipped school, one cop said to the other, and thought I hadn't heard. I felt sick and trapped worse than a chained prisoner and started thinking stupidly: What if I would have taken a piss a minute earlier or taken a different route home? You can spend your whole life taking different routes, avoiding one hell for another, almost finding paradise, *almost*, then realizing that your residence was fixed, defined despite you.

The surgeons, I was told numerous times, as if it were a goddamn class lesson, had managed to save my right arm, but it wasn't much use after that. A reminder. A huge string tied around my psyche. A mutely cooperative subject to be reflected in a mirror and painted again and again until the likeness was better than any real arm. My leg needed surgical work also, and its function returned, somewhat modified. A limp I never lost. Sometimes I exaggerate my limp for the hell of it. Not a lie, merely a little performance to alter the tedium in between paintings, or maybe it's a concession to what I was before the shooting. My dear limp. Another reminder. (Five years ago, I put together a show made up entirely of paintings of injured arms and legs, the wounds and scars graphic, the pain evident and incurable. And wouldn't you know it, overpriced as those paintings were, every damn one sold.) I was lucky to be alive—how many times did I hear that hollow phrase that spring and summer of recovery and personal transformation—but I didn't fight the phrase enough, started to believe it. *I was lucky*. My medical records will attest to that. I knew about the first three bullets. A fourth bullet, I was solemnly informed by a doctor I later painted in the most grim paleness, had grazed my skull when I was already unconscious, and he pointed to the corresponding spot on his own head. A half-inch over and I would have been . . .

My story certainly captured my hometown's imagination and heart. After all, we were an affluent, peaceful suburb not used to the gunning down of a teenager on a late spring afternoon. So what that I had a hammerlock on delinquency. I was nearly buried in get-well cards and gifts and the outpourings of well-wishers. A scholarship fund was set up for me, never mind that my parents were not hurting for cash. (I used the money, a few years later, to go to art school. By then I hated to miss a class, was an exemplary student. By then I was on my way, something of an artistic sensation.) Whoever had taken the four shots at me was never found or identified, despite, according to the police, a search that left no stone unturned, no clue neglected. A big reward was offered and reasons sought for the afternoon shooting, by the police and the media and parents, as though frantic philosophers were searching for the true meaning of existence. If the reasons could be found, maybe the bullets could be withdrawn, removed from flesh and time, who knows what their futile scurrying about indicated.

My summer was ruined, that was my early assessment during those first few months, moaned through my displacement and pain. Later, in retrospect, I started to say that it had been a great summer, the best summer of my life. Battling against the discomfort and boredom, I began to read in hospital; not only to read on my own, but I was read to by all sorts of sympathetic people, including a journalist who had left our friendly manicured suburb years before, but returned especially to meet and interview me. The journalist wrote a long article about the courageous, spunky young man and his horrifying ordeal. The article was published in a national magazine and won her some kind of important award for human-interest journalism. She always kissed me on the cheek when she arrived and before she left my hospital room—and she visited me often that summer, research and friendship—and once, after fantasizing about it night after night in my confinement, I turned my head and kissed her full on the lips. She smiled, called me a rambunctious boy, and kissed me back on the lips. That part wasn't in the magazine article. (I have four paintings of the journalist, her lipstick luminous in each. When my career was starting to take off, I looked her up but what I hoped for didn't happen. She was fifty then, and her marriage, she claimed, meant too much to her even to consider sleeping with me. We talked about those hospital kisses, that kiss, screwed with words for an afternoon, but that was all. I showed her some slides of the paintings I had done of her from memory, and she bought two of the oils, so the visit had not been all unprofitable fantasy pursuit.)

But getting shot and blind luck and prayers by strangers weren't what turned me around. The hospital had a wonderful rehabilitation program, and I learned to write and paint with my left hand. The art was therapeutic at first. Then it turned passionate, obsessive, as if painting were my inescapable calling, the shooting part of an elaborate plan to get me on a predetermined and constructive path. One of the nurses good-naturedly bought my first painting—of the dog that had sniffed my bloodied body—enough money for me to purchase a dozen comic books in the hospital gift shop. Then doctors and other nurses and visitors and staff started to buy anything I did, something of a game at the start, charitable, compassionate concern, like buying lemonade from a cute but scruffy kid at a corner stand. Eventually the realization that there was talent. Talent at the center of the bull's-eye some hidden, unseen assailant had hit close to dead center. (The real money didn't come till later, along with the successful shows and prestigious galleries and important art dealers, a whole different world I had no trouble handling, secretly enjoyed. I never had any big problem selling my work. I was spoiled in that respect. Very few setbacks as I established a reputation, in time became part of the art establishment. The publicity certainly didn't hurt, stayed with me, and I had to expend a minimum of energy promoting myself. Someone else was always more than willing to take care of publicizing me—a tradition started with the journalist that spring and summer of the shooting. But the talent was there. The talent at the center of the bull's-eye.)

I wind up sitting at the bar in an upscale air-conditioned lounge, thirty years later, in a different city, telling myself that my art requires a little lubrication, an artistic career has to be worked at in many ways, and an old man sits down next to me, stares in my direction, and says with soft-spoken eloquence, "I shot you, Derrick." The man was grey-haired authentic enough to be on a poster advertising kindly grandfathers. I wanted not to believe him, but I knew he had been the one, knew as well as I did my own name. He looked at my useless right arm, made a movement to touch it, but stopped, his hands trembling. It's part of me, don't get all upset, I told the old man, my first words to him.

I didn't want to know why he had tried to kill me thirty years before, and that was all he lived for now, to tell me the reason. We were sudden, mortal adversaries, despite his pathetic, helpless expression. All my painting, my entire artistic career, was somehow related to me not knowing, thinking instead about the shooting and what happened afterwards, trying artistically and imaginatively to comprehend and deal with the goddamn senselessness. *Unknown Assailant Paintings. The Body Damaged Paintings. Ordinariness Disturbed Paintings. The Sense of Senselessness Paintings. The Afternoon of My Rebirth Paintings.* . . . I like to paint in series, thematic connections, whether imposed or coming together naturally. Five or six or seven paintings to a series. Large, bold, unafraid paintings. Three or four or five series a year. I'm miserable when I'm not painting, terrified of the unproductive periods, so I do anything to keep working. Over seven hundred canvases completed in the last thirty years, not counting all the sketches and drawings and other artistic projects I've done. All related to what had happened. To not knowing.

I told the man that he didn't have to tell me anything, not even his name—I didn't care, he was forgiven. But he squeezed his liquor glass and told me that he was seventy-nine, almost eighty, and needed some comfort for his soul before—Before what? I asked. Before I meet my Maker, he said. You're my maker, I thought, hated the thought, wanted to scream the old man into oblivion. "Derrick," he said to me, as if I were a goddamn fourteen-year-old boy, then told me in a sad, worn, frightened voice, "I thought you were another kid. His father ruined my business. Cheated me. Drove me bankrupt. I'm sorry for hurting you. Terribly, terribly sorry." After coughing in helplessness, with tears in his eyes, this seventy-nine-year-old stranger, faceless resident of more dreams and nightmares than I care to remember, handed me a thick white rectangular envelope and said, "I know I can't repay you for what I did, but please accept this money. I was able to begin putting my life back together after that day."

That day. The start of *my* life. I took the envelope, saw my name scrawled on the outside, but left it unopened. I knew that the old man wanted me to open the envelope, to count the money. The counting would be close enough to forgiveness. My saying I forgave him wasn't good enough, nothing but empty absolution.

With a disconcerting sincerity, he declared, "Shooting you was the only bad thing I've done in my whole life. I've never stolen or lied to anyone."

"Have you ever seen anything I've painted?" I asked, wondering if he had the slightest idea of what was inside me. (I had drawn or painted dozens of people with guns, aiming or shooting from afar, their faces always indistinguishable. The beauty was in the anonymity and mysteriousness. The blood was unsurpassingly rich, my most articulate color. I had superb control of my pain, my past, my brush strokes.)

"I saw some of your beautiful paintings in art magazines. Never in person, I'm sorry to say," he admitted now, and rubbed his moist eyes, half in confusion, half in weariness, until he was able to go on: "I will now, I promise. Before I die. Before I meet my Maker."

I put the envelope down on the bar counter and used a felt-tip pen to sketch on a napkin as the old man continued to talk, sounding to me like he was confessing and explaining and pleading all at once. It was a sketch of him thirty years younger, a despondent man of forty-nine. I saw how he had looked, as if time had stopped and I was having a mystical vision. I signed the quickly completed sketch and gave it to the old man, having to press the napkin into his trembling hand. For the envelope full of money, I said, not knowing how much was in it.

While he was still admiring the sketch I picked up the envelope and started to walk out of the lounge, my limp undiminished, my right arm dangling unaltered at my side, yet cursing the truth and hoping I could paint from the lie that had been my life for thirty years.

I had talent, I assured myself, when I opened the door to the street and the summer heat hit my face. I had talent, I whispered firmly, and began to count the money in the envelope as I hurried away from the lounge in which my assailant sat, making my limp as noticeable as possible.

JOHN MANESIS

THE AILING POEM

The poem was overwhelmed
by all my trusted therapies,
weighted down with attention
and unnecessary medication,
never allowed to free itself
of its restraints, to rise
on its own from the sickbed,
perhaps to even levitate.

And in the end,
or was it the beginning,
I could not bring myself
To bury the ailing poem.
I salvaged a phrase or two,
set flame to what remained
and fanned the fire
with all my breath.

DON THACKREY

THE VERSE ROUNDUP

A herd of words drifts restless on the page,
Uncertain how to bunch or where to go.
It happens then that some few disengage
Themselves, with others following in tow.
The herd begins to move—haphazardly?—
Perhaps toward pastures not yet clearly seen
But somehow sensed to be synecdoche
For soul, for sustenance—for something green.
Then rhyming rides the point, and guides the herd,
With meter keeping order on the flanks.
Each noun and verb moves toward a partner word;
All join with others then in careful ranks.
Composing verse: a roundup of a kind,
A cattle-drive that happens in the mind.

FENCE FOR VERSE

I reckon you've heard about the rancher who
Writes sonnets while he tends his Angus herds.
That's me. The jobs are much alike, those two:
I fence in cows—I do the same with words.
Corralled, the critters have their proper use.
A fence—poetic form—holds words in check.
Like cows, words need protection, not turned loose
In fields to founder, or to run break-neck.
I choose each calf and test it as it grows
To join the herd, substantial, sleek, purebred.
Just so with words: idea embryos
That do the job or get culled out instead.
I want my cattle—and my verse—to stand
Steady, range-lean, clear-eyed—and show my brand.

PAUL HOSTOVSKY

THE CAT IS SLEEPING ON A DRAFT OF THIS POEM

that doesn't have a cat in it
though it does have
some children and some dogs
and some old ideas about the world
as it was.
As it is, the cat has no idea—
she simply padded over to the page
where she sensed some center was
or had been
or would be again,
and without insinuating herself
and without inserting herself
she sat on it
and like an onset
of warm summer rain
started washing herself
with the darting pink washcloth
of her tongue impinging
on every square inch
of the field, every grass blade,
every tree-branch, leaf, mailbox, huddled house,
and all the old ideas
which are getting warmer,
getting warmer,
and also the children and the dogs
who just kept running and playing together
as if they would remain
children and dogs forever.

HANNAH THOMASSEN

ORANGE MARMALADE CAT

Sees through the dark, makes rounds 24/7.
Comments on virtues and flaws. Long on the flaws.

Sits on my keyboard, contemplates possibilities.
Transmits.

That's odd, he might purr. *I usually like haiku.* Or,
That's odd, I don't usually like haiku.

Languishes on pages he likes, and those he does not.
Swishes his tail: *you're the poet, you decide.*

Bites and scratches me awake. Smirks.
Leaves dead stuff on my unimaginative doorstep.

Curls up on my chest, brings forth the heart
that lives there with the fear.

Points out it's all about rest and unrest most of the time
in that not-orange, not-yellow gold place.

I give him a squeeze, he gives back, scent of tangerine,
a spiral of rind,

and each little section in its delicate skin
into the palm of my hand.

TOM LESKIW

SMASHING THE BOX

Although I've dabbled in fiction, I consider myself a nonfiction writer. Often, the inspiration for my work springs from an outdoor experience while birding, hiking, or boating. However, my near-absolute allegiance to writing about the natural world sometimes causes me to reflect on the fine line that can separate a groove from a rut.

I joined a writer's group a little more than a year ago. Other members of the group often tackle genres and situations foreign to my own experience: gritty, sometimes macabre noir mysteries; zombie-esque apocalypses; elaborate, engrossing tales of fantasy; period pieces set in Europe and elsewhere; and essays that reflect on the interpersonal dynamics encountered in the corporate world or teaching profession. It's not that their work doesn't move me. Quite the contrary. I'm impressed and a bit envious of writers who can create something from nothing . . . or at least something beyond their own first-hand experiences. Although I have an unpublished novel and a long-neglected outline for another work of fiction, time and again, I find myself returning to the natural world for inspiration.

Inspection + reflection = inspiration is a familiar formula to my writing. However, the mere act of writing these words makes me want to escape from this self-constructed creative gulag for . . . er, if not greener pastures, something exotic—topics I've yet to explore.

For the science-based writing I do, I need to stay true to the facts; the natural world contains boundaries that I must always acknowledge. I can't give a character long-range views through a leafless hardwood forest in mid-summer. Or claim that returning adult salmon, far from the ocean, have shimmering silver bodies, when, in fact, their bodies are riddled with the black-and-white fungus of decay. To do so would mean that my writing has lost its tether to the natural world.

How I choose to interpret the same or similar event can spawn a variety of responses from me over time. How an experience is framed: which aspect is fore-grounded and which I relegate to the background makes all the difference. For instance, the passing of an elderly, beloved pet—experienced when one is six years old versus sixty—conjures different take-home lessons. To the elderly, seeing or experiencing another's death recalls the Russian proverb: *The fall of a leaf is a whisper to the living.* Whereas, a family dog's death seen through the eyes of youth likely serves as a first glimpse of mortality. It serves notice that the road doesn't run on forever. Yet the lesson isn't internalized; death is still an abstraction to the young. The consequences only apply to someone else. How could it be otherwise when children are preoccupied with springtime waves of green grass rippling in the breeze, or the joy of playing in a pile of autumn leaves?

There are no simple answers to the twin questions "Is creativity something that only takes root, flourishes, within bounds?" and "Is this a stance that limits or liberates?" My near-absolute allegiance to nonfiction has been an ongoing issue in my life. I carry this I-gotta-be-me stance too far, though. While others are having fun, adopting the persona of their chosen Halloween costume for the night, my friends know I'll muster only a tepid effort to temporarily inhabit another body. *I'll be Bruce Springsteen, circa 1984. Slip into jeans, grab a red bandanna from my sock drawer, and I'm good to go. No muss, no fuss. It's either that or stay home.*

Recently, however, I made a vow. Not only to think outside the box, but also to revel in smashing and incinerating that box altogether. To step outside the writing bounds I've created: non-fiction, always a point-of-view in the first person, and dealing only in scenarios supported by physics and reason. So, here goes:

The Aviator

Daylight came to the island of Kauai. The wind was slightly out of the west on that day, Monday, May 3, 1998. The Lihue airport was hectic, with a number of arrivals and departures scheduled. The aviator prepared for her return to Alaska. She'd done the run only once before, in the opposite direction. Clouds shifted and a shaft of sunlight knifed through, bathing the grasslands surrounding the tarmac in a hazy pink glow. All had been made ready. With resolute purpose, the aviator took off. Slowly, she rose to her cruising altitude and settled in for the long journey.

The sky, clear at the airport, began to fill with approaching cirrus clouds, portending a storm. Although the weather continued to worsen, the next several hours passed without incident. The wind—initially out of the west—shifted to out of the north. Heavy rain persisted throughout the next day; the aviator could feel the unceasing push of the strong north wind. Mindful of its effect on her course, she made a flight path correction, to the northwest. Despite this, the pounding rain and gale-force winds conspired to force her ever eastward: further and further off course.

Finally, the aviator glimpsed land. She was cold, tired, low on fuel. Approaching the coastline, she noted the details of the landscape: rocky point, grassy headland, cove. Suddenly, she was seized by a thought: I don't recognize this place. However, she could little afford the time for such a question. Her first priority was to land and fuel up. The aviator reduced her altitude, nearly colliding with . . .

A tall, two-legged creature. Startled, she wheeled and emitted a sharp cry, Chiu-eet, before finally alighting upon a steep, gravel-and-sand beach. She searched her memory for a recollection of the tall one. Yes . . . she'd seen several of his kind from afar during the past several months she'd spent in the mowed grasslands near the Lihue airport. The creature gestured wildly to his companion. Through the howling wind, the exhausted shorebird heard the creature shout, "Look! That one has a cinnamon rump!"

Thus began an unprecedented event: a fallout of bristle-thighed curlews along the Washington, Oregon, and northern California coast.

XXXX

Well, I tried, I really did. To concoct a story, to build a fictional world that lies beyond the bounds of my own experience. I've failed, for the truth is this:

An air of mystery surrounds the bristle-thighed curlew. Science has known something of the winter distribution of the species for quite some time, as the species was first described in 1785 by a naturalist aboard Captain Cook's ship while in Tahiti. However, more than a century and a half later, this enigmatic shorebird was the lone species in North America whose breeding location remained a mystery. It wasn't until 1948 in Alaska, near the mouth of the Yukon River, a curlew nest with four eggs was located by David Allen and Henry Kyllingstad. Newspaper headlines proclaimed: *163-Year Search Ends in Alaska.*

The geographic scope of the bristle-thighed curlew's migration astounds:

from Polynesia to Alaska, across open ocean. Until recently, it was not known whether those curlews that winter south of the main Hawaiian Islands stop to rest and feed there for a time before continuing their migration. Studies of marked birds have confirmed that they are capable of overflying the main islands, resulting in a nonstop route of 5,500 miles. Because of their migration route, far from any continental land mass, the species had been recorded along the west coast of North America south of Alaska prior to 1998 on only one occasion: May 31, 1969 on Vancouver Island, British Colombia.

Then, during late April 1998, an immense low-pressure system formed—then stalled—off the coast of southern Oregon. Beginning in late April, Alaskan-bound curlews flew directly into this low-pressure cell, and its strong, northerly air flow. On May 6, Dave Lauten posted an Internet message to an Oregon bird chat group that he and Kathy Castelein had possibly seen a bristle-thighed curlew at Floras Lake, near New River in Curry County. Two days later, two of the birds were discovered at Point Brown Jetty at Grays Harbor, Washington. The next day, two were detected at the South Jetty of the Columbia River.

✕✕✕

On May 14, the first bird was reported in California by Alan Barron at the Battery Point lighthouse in Crescent City. Never having before seen this species—despite searching for it on several islands of the Hawaiian chain—several companions and I traveled to Crescent City. There, in a vacant lot with discarded concrete rubble and feral cats, rested the bird. Oblivious to the burgeoning crowd of bird enthusiasts, it wandered slowly about the unkempt grass, feeding and preening its feathers. We marveled at the bird's landfall, consulted our field guides, and documented its presence with photographs. This bird was considered by experts to be one of fifteen to twenty-five that made it to the West Coast during spring 1998.

I tried to imagine the sequence of events that had conspired to misdirect these birds to the West Coast. As the seasons shifted and the number of hours of daylight each day increased, flocks of curlews experienced an urge for going, known as *zugunruhe*—a seasonally occurring restlessness that immediately preceded their migration. The turn of the seasons affects humans as well. Songwriter and musician Joni Mitchell explored the sensation—albeit autumnal rather than vernal—in her song "Urge for Going."

Prior to the advent of agriculture, a twice yearly human migration was the norm in many places: to the mountains in summer to escape the valley heat, then return in the fall, to flee winter's grip. Genetic memory runs deep, which explains our inherent autumnal restlessness, the urge to follow flocks of migrating birds to someplace warm and alive. Legions of "snowbirds" submit twice yearly to this urge for going. In the northern hemisphere, their fall journey is an example of "human heliotropism"—bending toward the increased light of lower latitudes.

Now that I'm retired, Joni's words have a special resonance, as my wife Sue and I spend the winter in sunny Arizona. During March, lengthening hours of daylight portend the arrival of spring, which prompts our desire to return north. About a month later, in preparation for their departure from Tahiti, bristle-thighed curlews abandon their winter territory. Milling about with others, they ready themselves for the trip north. And so it is for snowbirds, too. Packed and ready, we join the surging tide northward.

Imagine a jet flying non-stop from San Francisco to New York City . . . and nearly back again. This is the one-way distance the bristle-thighed curlew covers. The bird's arduous migration over inhospitable open ocean—offering no food or respite—inspires awe. In 1948, Arthur A. Allen, the leader of the expedition to pin-point the nesting grounds of the bristle-thighed curlew, marveled at their tenacity:

> *Why these curlews should want to leave the warm, luxurious shores of Tahiti and the other South Sea islands, fly 5,500 miles over the open sea, and arrive at one of the most forlorn stretches of tundra in North America, deserted by all other birds and still largely covered by snow, just to lay four eggs, is hard to understand.*

As wildlife biologist and writer Scott Weidensaul observed in *Living on the Wind*, "Bird migration is the world's only true unifying natural phenomenon, stitching the continents together in a way that even the great weather systems fail to do." For birders, the opportunity to study a bristle-thighed curlew along the Pacific Coast transcends the mere act of seeing a bird. A veil's been lifted. We've glimpsed—and in doing so, been woven into—a vast and mysterious world-wide tapestry, if only for a few hours.

PETRA DAI WALECH

AND A PIECE OF THE WALL FALLS THROUGH . . .

When a piece of the wall falls
We patch it with tin
We cake it with mud
Or straw
Until the wind can't take us anymore

)(

Calloused hands reach up to our brow
Wiping grease and blood and rust
Our fingernails are clipped close to the flesh
Dust has settled into the lines of our palms
Cheap soaps only smear hard work across our backs

)(

At the sound of the alarm
we rise
And at the end of the day
we fall
Into our beds

)(

Those who came before us told us to listen
To those who came before them
To wake promptly
To mend the wall
To wash promptly
To sleep
To pass along what we learn to our children

)(

The wall is weak in certain spots
But we do not let it fall
The wall falls down
But we do not let it die
The wall falls onto us while we save it from gravity
And time
And wind and rain and erosion
And we find our mother's teeth
And we find our father's jaw
We find ourselves devoid of ceremony
And the shovels take our mother's teeth and our father's jaw
They are tossed away
And we go to sleep and forget

)(

Sleep is stale air sucked through nostrils
Rejected by our bodies
Released through open mouths
Moans escape unintelligible
And we are stiff and cold when we wake

)(

As the sun builds our thoughts focus on work
And we ready ourselves for tin and mud and straw
To see where the wall could fall
So we suck down black coffee
And we try to speed up
Fingers twitching we slip on gloves
Fingers twitching we drop our shovel
Fingers twitching and we go to the wall

𝕏

We do not do our work our best today and we are sent home early
And we are tired and lay down in bed
We forget to wash and scrub
The sheets are smeared with dirt and sweat
We think we should clean up
But something is tugging at the back of our skull
And instead of grabbing the cheap soap
We pull the blankets over our head
And soon we are drifting

𝕏

We are dreaming now and this is a dream
Heavy clumps of dirt hang from our arms
Our hair is heavy and our heads bowed
Our knees are bent
And our feet are sore
We smell blood, no iron, no sweat
And suddenly the smell is overwhelming

𝕏

We wake with sickness thick in the air
We are not well
Inhalation the doctor says
Wear a mask
You will heal
Sleep the doctor says

𝕏

When we are better we return to work
But our nerves are damaged
We shake sometimes
Like we are afraid
Maybe we are but we do not know anymore
We like to sleep

ᚷ

Tonight is the same as all the rest we are clean for bed and wait to fall away
Our fingers curl from the memory of things our fathers and our mothers
carried home to us while we were asleep in our beds
They taught us to carry on the memory of their own faults and their own
pain and so we continue to patch the wall
Even though all we want to do is dream
But all that comes is sleep
And at the alarm our thoughts are only of the wall

BARBARA CROOKER

WEATHER REPORT

All this time on the planet, and still I am no wiser
than I was thirty years ago, when I began to write,
scratching on a yellow pad while the voices in my head
screeched *not good enough*. They're still shrieking
their shrill words in my left ear, just above the migraine
that's singing a high E sharp from its perch in my brain.
Not good enough, and I know it, but today the sky
is that low blue note that comes after a storm,
and the locust is sending out round green messages
as it bobs and weaves in the wind. There's a flock
of cedar waxwings in the sumac, wearing
their little black masks, stealing the afternoon away.
The light streams in from the west, still I wrestle
with my old friends faith and doubt. A thin scribble
of clouds floats by, obscuring the sky, and all the words
are hiding, elusive as that bird over there, the one
that's singing its heart out, just out of sight.

LE TEMPS PERDU

I'm sitting here in this green glade, trying to write, at a wrought iron table
patterned with roses, but I'm empty of words, a dictionary of blank pages,
a pen out of ink. Sunlight is filtering through a thousand tiny leaves,
seeping down to the grass and ivy, like sitting in a cup of green tea.
All I can do is burble mindlessly, like the house wrens and robins,
haunted by the ghosts of what I've written here, other times. I'm sure
the Chinese philosophers have a name for this, revisiting a place of former
happiness that you can never recapture. The cardinal keeps singing *compare,
don't compare*, and a squirrel runs up the path, cracks a nut in his sharp little
teeth. Something wonderful is just about to happen.

HANNAH THOMASSEN

ADVICE FOR OLD POETS

Don't look back.
Remember everything.
Write your poems.

Don't look back.
Remember everything.
Write your poems.

Don't look ahead.
The end of the road
will spill over the horizon soon enough.
.

Look in the mirror. Your face is testimony.
If asked, say you are Witness.
Say you are Center, you hold the storm.

When the wind is bewitched
and when it is not, the storm is,
and will be, when you are not.

God was of no consequence.
God was Lover. Demon. Nothing at all.
Once, the forest was God.

Write your poems.

IV
ARTISTS' LIVES

MICHELE MARKARIAN

STARS OF THE STARTUPS

Jeanne stared at the haiku that had just been handed back to her by her editor.

She'd been assigned to write a puff piece on some twenty-five-year-old hotshot who dropped out of UPenn to start a company called Blade Razor, which was some sort of shaving and grooming app for corporate hipsters too busy to remember. Devon Royd, the hotshot, was pretty colorless and didn't have a lot to say for himself. Jeanne was wondering how she was going to crank out one of *Stars of the Startups* infamous formulaic profiles—upbringing, school, first job, aha moment, paydirt!—with someone so monochromatic when inspiration took hold.

> *Devon Royd is young*
> *With a voice like flat soda.*
> *How come he is rich?*

"Jeanne, what's this?" asked Maya Sloan-Banarjee, *Stars of the Startups's* editor, after Jeanne had put it on her desk. "Is this some kind of joke? I mean, it's funny, but—"

"I think it's apt," said Jeanne. "Maya, you should have seen this guy—talk about boring! He wouldn't open up about anything. I had to practically pull the words out of him—"

"It's your job to make him open up," said Maya curtly. "Submit a real profile, please. You know the drill."

In an instant Jeanne had her own aha moment—this job was holding her back, stifling her creativity. My God, she was a writer, and writers were supposed to tell the truth, weren't they? So maybe it wasn't one of her better haiku, but at least it was more honest than glossing over someone's personality with hype.

"I have to go. I forgot I have a doctor's appointment," Jeanne lied, grabbing her purse and heading towards the door.

"What about—" she heard Maya say to her retreating back.

"I'll get it to you later," said Jeanne, before texting her best friend Jarvis and asking him to meet her for a drink.

"I hope it's someone who specializes in improving one's writing," called Peter Piedmont, another staff writer and Jeanne's nemesis. Peter was overweight, unhappy and asexual. He and Jeanne, in the three years they'd worked together, had yet to engage in banter that wasn't laced with hostility.

"I'll get you a referral if it is," snapped Jeanne as she exited.

)()()(

A half hour later, Jeanne found herself sitting across from Jarvis at the Buddha Bar, a bottle of white wine chilling between them.

"You can't leave. You have the best job," sighed Jarvis, an unemployed architect and serial housesitter.

"Jarvis, you of all people. I thought you believed in me," said Jeanne, pouring herself some more wine.

"Sweetheart, you know I believe in you, but how are you going to live?" Jarvis scanned his iPhone for emails. He had recently sent out a spate of resumes, and was waiting on a response. "Nothing. Letters to Santa, every last one."

"But Jarvis, at least you have time for your art," said Jeanne.

"What art? I'm so goddamn worried about money I can't even afford supplies!" snapped Jarvis.

"We'll have time to do *The Artist's Way* together. We can meet for artist dates. You just need someone to get you going," encouraged Jeanne.

"We've already done *The Artist's Way*. Twice," said Jarvis.

"Yeah, but only on the weekends. Now—"

"Jeanne, what is this about?" asked Jarvis. "It can't be about a stupid haiku. That's just dumb. You know damn well you've written better things than that."

"Well, it's kind of about the haiku," said Jeanne. "Not this particular haiku—I agree, it could be better. But why not a haiku? Why does every stupid profile have to have the same stupid format? What's the point of—"

"Because it sells, that's why," said Jarvis. "And the more it sells, the better the company does and the better you do."

"Jarvis, I'm talking about my soul," cried Jeanne. She could tell she was getting buzzed by the edge of hysteria creeping into her voice. "I'm a sellout, man. A total sellout, interviewing people who are following their bliss while I languish in nine-to-five world."

"Please. They're probably all trust funders," said Jarvis morosely. Trust funders were a topic of particular distress for Jarvis. Jeanne knew she had to steer the conversation back on track before things took a wrong turn.

"Follow your bliss," Jeanne chanted. "Do what your heart dictates and the money will follow. Or something like that."

"That's crap and you know it," sighed Jarvis. "Besides, you get a lot of good material from your job."

"Like what? Not this latest whizkid, let me tell you."

"Like—what about that short story you wrote about the intern a few summers ago? What was her name? Lily?" Jarvis checked his iPhone again, groaned, and snapped it shut.

"Lily. Lily the Lionhearted." Jeanne smiled as she remembered the intern whose scrappy demeanor had inspired her to write a children's story. Granted, she had done nothing with the story—she should have shopped it around—but who had time?

"I would love to illustrate that for you," said Jarvis.

Jeanne leaned forward. "Why didn't you say so?"

Jarvis shrugged. "I don't know. I always thought you'd ask, and you never did."

"Oh my God, Jarvis, that's a great idea!" cried Jeanne.

"I know," said Jarvis. "Kind of like *The Artist's Way*, only real."

"That can be your artist date! The illustration! And what can mine be?" mused Jeanne.

"Shut up and go back to work," said Jarvis.

)X()X(

Jeanne tiptoed into the office a few hours later, after treating herself to a window shopping spree down Newbury Street. It was somewhat of a failed trip, as payday wasn't for another week and the bottle of wine had cost Jeanne more than she'd anticipated.

"I smell a brewery," said Peter.

"I smell ass," whispered Jeanne.

"Finish your piece on Mr. Devon Royd yet?"

"In my sleep," retorted Jeanne. She sat at the computer and thought about how to make Devon Royd interesting. It wasn't going to be easy.

Out of the corner of her eye, she saw Peter staring at his own computer. He had stuck a pencil in his ear, and was twirling it. He examined the end with his fingers, then wiped it on his pants.

You are so gross, thought Jeanne. The modern, unappealing version of J. Alfred Prufrock. She imagined Peter in love with Devon and not being able to do anything about it. This almost made her feel sorry for him.

Devon Royd is not what you would expect from an Internet tycoon, she typed. Jeanne remembered the smart-looking handbag she'd seen on Newbury Street. Maybe after next payday, if she decided to stay, she could buy it.

"Everything okay here?" asked Maya, coming over to Jeanne's desk and smiling. "You okay?"

"Sure she is. There's a bar in her doctor's office!" beamed Peter. Maya gave Jeanne a concerned look and walked away.

Average height, average build, unassuming mien, she typed while stealing a glance at Peter. Maybe it was Maya he was in love with. Maybe he'd been sitting there for three years, pining away for a woman who was not only his boss, but married?

Jeanne took out a notebook. "Peter/Devon. Peter/Maya" she wrote. She would play with these later, when she got home. *Who would guess from his Clark Kent looks that an entire generation of men would be relying on his app, Blade Razor, for good grooming?* With a little imagination Jeanne could finish this piece quickly and start thinking about the possibilities.

MIKE MAGGIO

ATELIER

She goes with him. He is very nice, it seems. His face is finely chiseled. His eyes, deep and dark, are intense and penetrating. What you'd expect, she thinks, though his hands are big and strong, too big, it seems, for such fine, delicate work. Though there are still traces of paint on his fingers, under his nails where he has tried very hard to remove the streaks of yellow, red and magenta.

She goes with him to his atelier. Even though they have only met. Even though she knows she must be careful in this city where no one is safe. You could be mugged or raped, or even worse, in this city where she lives and works.

But he has made her laugh, and she has not laughed for some time now, not since she became alone again, some six months ago, when her last lover took suddenly to the wind. Things became too restrictive, it seems, and he had to go. At least, that's what he said.

She goes with him because he, her new lover, was so kind when she tripped so clumsily at the bar—was it on purpose?, she wonders, she had noticed him, hadn't she?, was there some unconscious wish that things would take a turn to where they are leading now?—and he so politely, ever so gently helped her to her feet and smiled.

He smiled.

And then he introduced himself: "Collin. Collin Spears."

And it was a shock to her, really, like when you accidentally touch a faulty appliance and you quickly pull back, only her reaction wasn't nearly so abrupt, for it had been so long since she had had to decide how to respond to someone who had smiled at her like that.

"Collin," he said. "Collin Spears."

"Are you all right?" he said.

But she was too busy standing up to reply, coordinating each muscle, each movement—it's not easy, you know—trying to manage her embarrassment, trying to coordinate her reaction to his kindness, that she could not answer, she could not even think to respond as the words penetrated the layers of her awareness: "Collin. Collin Spears."

It was as if a dream had overcome her, and the words were strange, evasive sounds that disassociated themselves from their source and took on a life of their own. She saw fields of snow bundled cozily into a picture-perfect scene, children snug in hats and muffs playing merrily, and there were bells jingling as a horse and sleigh slid quietly by carrying two lovers in a warm embrace.

Collin Spears. It was a cool, refreshing sound, a sprig of spearmint on a hot, humid day, anything but a man who had at once decided to look upon her with kindness. And then:

"Are you all right?"

Now she is with him. Catherine Whittaker. Legal secretary by day. Seeker of the heart by night. Walking through the broken, deserted streets in a part of town she has never been to. Her heart is pounding. She is anxious about her encounter with this man, this Collin Spears, she is somewhat frightened even, but her hand is in his, brings her back, ever so slightly, to reality, and she glances at his tender face, silhouetted against the harsh streetlight, his handsome, well-trimmed beard, and she decides his kindness is something she needs to risk at this very critical juncture in her life.

✕✕✕

Happiness is a difficult state to assess, she decides as she flips through the paintings—all of the same woman, she notes, his last lover, no doubt—that lie stacked against the walls of his atelier. Like trying to define a color, like trying to determine, for example, the very nature of blue which, through all its shades and manifestations—cobalt, azure, indigo—can never truly be blue no matter how hard it strives to be.

Nevertheless, she appears to feel something akin to happiness—a light, floating feeling, a feeling she could flit through his atelier like Tinker Bell, a feeling the figurines that line the walls could somehow whisper secret madrigals from their frozen faces—something as close to blue as one can possibly get, she thinks.

Catherine Whittaker, who has not known love for an eternity, it seems, who, having now been made love to, having been taken to the very moon which beams down through the skylight and rests serene across her new lover's face, examines Collin Spears with a jeweler's eye as he sleeps naked on the bed, and she wonders if this could be a hint of the truest blue ever imagined.

XOXOX

Soon she is modeling for him. Soon he convinces her to quit her job and remove her clothes—the very straight-laced receptionist now with her hair untied and flowing, posing this way and that.

Soon she comes to realize how remarkable he truly is with his gentle hands that shape her very existence on the canvas by day, which probe the very depths of her passion by night. His kindness is unending, his dark, mysterious temperament captures her soul and absorbs her slowly and completely into his.

Catherine Whittaker—girl from the farm, who left her family for a life far away in the city, who, against all odds, made it big of a fashion, did it all on her own, now after fifteen years, reaching new heights at this low point in her life—bares her body and her soul to Collin Spears, a successful, urban artist whose dexterous fingers redefine her on canvas and off.

Never afraid to take risks, never afraid to use his subjects to the utmost as the instruments of his genius, Collin Spears strips her bare, Catherine Whittaker, innocent country girl, goes to the very heart of her, transforms her into lines and colors, planes and shapes until the canvas becomes her—that spot a tear, that angle a heartbreak, that splash of red a deep, deep passion that longs to rise up. Until Catherine Whittaker becomes the canvas, her body capsulized into the two-dimensional space, her personality deconstructed, interpreted, transformed, her soul diffused into light and shadow.

Then, soon after, the initial days of blind wonderment end, soon she becomes just another fixture in his atelier—a painting, a figurine, an object frozen in space. Soon his atelier becomes filled with her—the canvases abound, the figurines he has made of her multiply, until she begins to lose all sense of herself, until she can no longer distinguish between image and reality. Catherine Whittaker the woman and Catherine Whittaker the subject merge into one, here in his atelier where Collin Spears manipulates her desires, where light and shadow play havoc with her senses, and eventually the initial joy fades into the background like an inexpensive poster whose colors wane under the unrelenting rays of the sun.

XOXOX

One day, he says to her: "I have finished my work."

It's a casual remark, over a cup of coffee, in a mug he has fashioned in her likeness.

He has painted all he can of her, he explains, he has sculpted every possible variation. He must move on to his next subject.

"You understand, of course."

"Of course," she answers, feeling rather numb, though she is not sure she really does, though she is sure she has heard something like this somewhere before.

He will never forget her, he continues, as if pressed. How could he?, he asks. She has become a permanent fixture in his atelier, has earned a permanent place within his heart.

Catherine Whittaker responds with a blank expression. She is not surprised, not upset, not anything really, for he has left her with nothing except the bare minimum of who she once was.

She surveys his atelier. Her image hangs in every corner, the three-dimensional figurines he has made of her sit in every nook and cranny. They are strange and foreign, nothing like what she thinks she remembers of herself, they are like flakes of skin she has unwillingly shed.

She carefully examines each one. She wants to find a clue, some fragment that will indicate who she might be.

She dismisses the paintings. She has grown tired of the garish colors, the harsh thick brush strokes he used on her face, the complicated planes of light he constructed where her body should have been.

She goes instead to the figurines, each with a different expression, each a window to a moment of her past. She hopes they will speak to her, hopes she will discover a sneer or a grimace that will help her understand how she is feeling at this very moment.

But they stare back at her, glum and silent, like ghosts that are unable even to haunt her. Their faces are blank, though they seem to wish to sing, to speak, to scream something secret to her that she must now absolutely know.

Then it comes to her, a tiny glimpse of the past, a vague echo that rises up within.

She raises her head, looks at the man sitting before her, sipping his coffee in a cup shaped in her likeness. Her eyes sparkle momentarily as she recollects.

"I knew a man once," she says at last. "His skin was warm like fresh cow's milk. His touch was like goose down. His voice was the gentle cooing of a dove. He used to paint dreams," she says. "I could get lost in them if I let myself. I believe I am lost in one now."

She puts her hands to her face, her arms, her body, as if she is not quite sure whether she is awake.

She smiles.

"Collin," she says. "His name was Collin Spears."

"I am he," he says.

"Oh," she says, and she wakes up. "I must go now."

"Yes," he says, his face suddenly gone sad. "You must go."

"Can you find your way out?" he asks.

Catherine Whittaker collects herself from about the room like a school girl collecting leaves. She gathers her clothes, the trinkets she brought with her when she first moved in, all the possessions she has accumulated and saved since the day she came to the city.

"Yes," she answers. "I believe I have been here before."

"I believe I will never be here again," she says.

She smiles, a kind, simple, tranquil smile.

Collin Spears turns his face away. He gets up. One by one, he removes her paintings, stacks them up, against the wall. It is a ritual he has practiced, to mark the end of each project.

Catherine Whittaker watches him as she walks toward the doorway. His hands tremble as he lifts each canvas. His face, long and worn, appears old in the harsh sunlight that filters through the skylight in his atelier.

"Are you all right?" she asks, as she turns the doorknob, as if that is the only thing left to say.

JOHN GREY

OF A WRITER AND HIS WIFE

I have a mistress in this study
and the smallest things anger her:
the loud whirr of your alarms
at toothpaste caked lime green in basins
or clothes strewn kamikaze
across the bedroom floor;
these appearances
at my door, expeditions
sent out from your world
of kitchen and parlor
to rescue your long lost husband;
even your presence
anywhere in the house,
sometimes nothing more
than the distant purr of a vacuum cleaner,
glasses clinking in a
dishwasher, the slap
of blankets across the bed.

She will not be content
until she has done away
with you altogether, your
order, your reason, your
connection to nuts and
bolts, to grease, to gravel.

My mistress and I make love
in a frantic boudoir of shiny white keys,
in a glowing screen,
on sheets of paper spat out
by the technology of my imagination,
our passion stirred to
pleasure pitch, to poetry.

And yet she can't steal
all of me, this cannonball of creative flesh.
She still looks up
when you stand in the door,
or cocks her ear at
the noises your life makes.
Truth is I love you more.
But I need her around
so that I'll have the words to tell you that.

ALAN SWYER

THE ORACLE

Warning signals were present right from the start.

"We love that little movie you made about baseball," said the emissary, an earnest sort named Herb Klein who was part of a group visiting Los Angeles for a few days.

"What little baseball movie?" Leibowitz asked.

"That exciting one that runs ten minutes or so."

"Except it's not a movie. It's a promo for the film I'm finishing."

"But what would it take to do something like that on meditation?"

"A promo?"

Herb Klein nodded.

"Same thing as with baseball," Leibowitz explained. "I'd have to shoot the film, then cut excerpts."

"You couldn't just—"

"Shoot ten minutes or so of footage?"

Again Herb Klein nodded, though with considerably less hope.

"In what you saw," Leibowitz said, "how many people are on screen?"

"At least ten."

"Try fifteen. If I'm going to shoot that many interviews, think it makes sense to get one sound byte per person? Except for post-production, it's no different than making a full-length film."

"L-let me get back to you," Herb Klein mumbled awkwardly.

꧁꧂꧁꧂

Since most overtures from outside the world of filmmaking inevitably proved to be what Leibowitz, in moments of kindness, termed *fishing expeditions*—and in less benevolent moments, *wheel-spinning, courtesies,* or *total fucking wastes of time*—he expected that the meditation project would vanish as surely and swiftly as those regarding kickboxing, sports nicknames, teaching experiences in Fiji, and the wonderful world of S&M.

Though the reasons given, in the few cases where further contact ensued, were various and sundry, the bottom line, Leibowitz knew full well, was invariably money. Talk was cheap, but not check-writing.

So Leibowitz was more than surprised when, a day later, Herb Klein asked to meet for a cup of tea.

"Tell me what it might take," Herb began when they sat down at a funky Santa Monica coffee house rumored to be owned by Bob Dylan.

"Money and freedom."

"How much?"

"Of which?

"Which one matters more?" Herb asked.

"The money matters, but not as much as the freedom."

"The Oracle is accustomed to complete control," Herb said, referring to the preferred name of his spiritual master.

"Then he can have it."

"Really?"

"Just not with me involved."

Looking pensive, Herb took a sip of his green tea. "Non-negotiable?" he asked.

"Deal-breaker. And a handshake's not enough. What's known as *Final Cut* has to be specified both in my contract and in paperwork with the Directors Guild."

"Let me see what I can do."

"And there's more. If you want a puff piece, count me out."

To Leibowitz's surprise, Herb Klein smiled. "I knew you were the right guy."

"Can I get that in English?"

"He's already commissioned films from a couple of people he could control."

"Misfires?"

"Disasters," Herb acknowledged with what Leibowitz took to be a hint of glee.

)()()(

Since Leibowitz was considered by many to be the consummate cynic, few even in his inner circle realized that he had an interest in Eastern spirituality dating all the way back to high school, when he first discovered

Jack Kerouac, Gary Snyder, and Alan Watts.

In the years that followed, Leibowitz spent a period of time with an Indian guru named Muktananda, then did a stint at a Zen center. Each experience, at some point, was short-circuited by two phenomena: Leibowitz's crazy work schedule, plus the squirming that resulted whenever he attempted to sit still on a cushion for a significant length of time.

The compromise, thanks to a woman in his life, came through technology. Though he jokingly referred to the approach as *The Lazy Man's Path To Enlightenment*, or *Beatitude Lite*, lying in bed with headphones on proved to be an effective means of escaping from the hubbub of life and finding a surprising degree of serenity.

In no time his CD collection, which featured the likes of Ray Charles, Nina Simone, Sonny Rollins, and Solomon Burke, grew to include a guided meditation by a Sri Lankan monk, a Delta wavelength album by an Orange County chiropractor, several questionable ventures into New Age music, and, ultimately, one about which he was initially apprehensive, since it was recorded by someone who called himself *The Oracle*.

That CD, which Leibowitz privately dubbed *Ory's Greatest Hits*, proved to be a mainstay once he overcame first the name, then his distrust of someone sporting what looked like a dead animal on his head.

)(X)(

The morning following his second rendezvous with Herb, Leibowitz was ushered into the Marina Del Ray hotel suite in which the visiting spiritual master was staying. After being served an unpalatable protein shake, he waited until the enlightened one emerged from the bedroom, wearing a pajama-like garment that looked like a reject from the Hugh Hefner collection.

"Herbie says you've hijacked my movie," said the man known as The Oracle.

"More like I'm coming to the rescue."

"Am I not the master?"

"Of meditation, maybe. But of film?"

"And you are?"

"Want to compare track records?"

"I'd say you've got a pugnacious side."

"Same as you."

The man known as The Oracle studied Leibowitz with his intense gaze, then nodded. "Before we go on, any questions?"

"What am I supposed to call you?"

"Anything wrong with The Oracle?"

"When we're sitting and talking? You bet."

"Then how about T.O.?"

"I didn't realize you were a wide receiver."

The Oracle's face went blank. "Is there something I'm missing?"

"That you're not a football fan. But let's turn things around. What questions do *you* have?"

"How do you see the movie about me?"

"I don't."

"B-but—"

"Herb told me it was about meditation."

"Isn't it the same thing?"

"Not as I understand it."

Leibowitz caught what he took to be a grimace from the man he was trying to think of as T.O. "Tell me what you envision," the holy man then asked.

"A fresh look at Eastern spirituality in the Western world."

"With?"

"Not just gurus, swamis, and *rinpoches*, but also scientists, physicians, scholars, and the like."

"And where do I fit in?"

"Isn't one judged by the company he keeps?"

"But in that company, how much screen time will I get?"

"I guess that depends on what you say and do."

"Which means, if I understand correctly, I can come up with the funding—"

"Yeah—"

"Then find myself on what I believe is known as the cutting room floor."

"Know what they say where I grew up in Jersey?" Leibowitz asked.

"Tell me."

"Sometimes life's a bitch."

✖✖✖

Accustomed to immersing himself in different worlds, Liebowitz, once given a *go-ahead* he wasn't sure would be forthcoming, huddled with an assistant. Together they assembled a *wish list* of people to interview, knowing full well that it was likely to grow exponentially as days turned to weeks, then weeks to months.

Leibowitz's *mantra* about the making of a documentary, to use a term he plucked from Eastern spirituality, was something he'd uttered spontaneously while doing a Q&A after a festival screening of a film he made about the criminal justice system. When asked if there was one special key, his reply was succinct. "You need to have a firm sense of the film you want to make," he began, "then hope you stumble upon a better one."

That certainly proved to be the case on what came to be known as "East Meets West." Virtually everyone he interviewed opened doors to other people and places. A psychiatrist in Lower Manhattan, whose writings attempted to reconcile the Buddha with Freud, led him to an institute at Harvard for the study of meditation and psychotherapy. The folks there, in turn, introduced him to a scientist whose high tech study of the cortex of meditators demonstrated that a steady practice slowed—and sometimes even reversed—the loss of neuroplasticity in the brain that led, among other things, to memory loss. That woman then put him in touch with a brilliant Sikh at Harvard Med School, whose work showed the benefits in stress reduction—plus mental and physical health—from a consistent practice of yoga and meditation.

A steady stream of airports followed as Leibowitz and his cameraman met with a Columbia professor who'd been initiated as a Lama by the Dalai Lama himself, an ex-Catholic priest who had switched spiritual paths, an American-born swami who ran an ashram in Oregon, then a woman known far and wide as the *Hugging Saint* of India.

Other interviews followed: a Zen master; a woman who introduced meditation, under the secular name *Mindfulness*, to classes of inner city kids; a Los Angeles psychiatrist who authored a paper about success treating ADHD with meditation rather than medication; and several Buddhist nuns.

New themes kept asserting themselves: how Eastern spirituality morphed when it reached Western shores; how it interacted—sometimes comfortably, sometimes less so—with medicine and science; how it could be incorporated into Western lifestyles; and, perhaps most interesting of all, how the role of women was evolving in what had been a largely patriarchal system.

✗✗✗

The non-stop travel, coupled with interviews that ranged from eye-opening to scintillating, proved to be a dizzying experience. But even as he reported in periodically, informing his benefactor about what had been said, and by whom, a question kept gnawing at Leibowitz. How would the man who billed himself as The Oracle, but who came off in person like a somewhat epicene song-and-dance man, fit in amongst such luminaries?

By the time Leibowitz made his way to The Oracle's compound in rural North Carolina—a place known as The Sanctuary—that question had blossomed into a full-blown obsession.

Gun shy, Leibowitz deferred what he sensed might be a showdown by spending a couple of days interviewing members of the adherents known as *The Flock*, not a single one of whom gave him even the slightest bit of comfort or hope. They were what he considered to be *the walking wounded—* the kind of people he'd encountered over the years in AA meetings and in cult-like groups—only with far less interesting tales to tell.

Nor was he encouraged when at last he sat down, with the camera running, with the spiritual master himself. Knowing that thanks to the wonders of editing he simply needed a handful of pithy sound bytes to create a positive image, Leibowitz found himself fighting against not just cliches like *bliss, transcendence,* and *the third eye,* but also the kind of gibberish generally mouthed by geeks who were eager to impress. *High-tech, cutting edge,* and *a marriage between ancient techniques and 21ˢᵗ century means,* Leibowitz knew too well, would come off on-screen as highfalutin, lame, and empty, especially when juxtaposed against the brilliance of the others who would be sharing screen time.

The problem was enough to cause a sleepless night. There would be no joy whatsoever in burning the man who had initiated a project he had come to care deeply about. But more importantly, thanks to his own personal experiences, he believed that despite the trite jargon, The Oracle's technology definitely worked.

✗✗✗

The only possible solution, Leibowitz realized as he found himself pacing at 4 a.m., would be to create a situation in which the world could see

The Oracle's technology in action, then witness the results for themselves.

But where could that be done? And how?

It was only at dawn, when Leibowitz was hiking through The Sanctuary's hills, that a thought materialized—one that might be hard to arrange, and which might cause The Oracle to balk.

ЖѺЖ

Without discussing his notion with the film's financing source, Leibowitz kept to himself until it was a reasonable hour to make some calls. Then, while waiting for a response, he took a drive into Chapel Hill so as to be neither visible nor accessible on The Sanctuary grounds until he hopefully had the kind of approval he was seeking.

ЖѺЖ

It was nearing dusk when Leibowitz drove up toward the building on the grounds of The Sanctuary that he had come to think of as the Inner Sanctum. Perched atop a hill, it was an overly decorated building that housed The Oracle's office and abode.

Taking off his shoes, Leibowitz was asked by a minion to wait, which he did while eying the *tchotchkes* that abounded: silly figurines, drawings, memorabilia, and gifts.

"So tell me about this brainstorm," The Oracle said as he entered the room together with a young male aide.

"You wanted to know what would separate you from the others seen on-screen."

"Indeed."

"For the most part, we'll only see them talking."

"Whereas I—?"

"Will be seen changing lives."

From the look on The Oracle's face, Leibowitz sensed that he had him.

ЖѺЖ

As he and The Oracle, in a rented PT Cruiser, approached a state prison in Northern New Jersey a week later, Leibowitz watched his passenger grow apprehensive.

"You okay?" Leibowitz asked.

"Everything is as it should be," replied The Oracle without much conviction.

Aware that, thanks to the strings he had been able to pull, Herb Klein and a Sanctuary helper had gone into the prison two hours earlier together with two crew members—the cinematographer and a sound man—Leibowitz chose not to press the issue.

After clearing a checkpoint and a metal detector, the two men were led to a room where, in addition to the two technicians, plus Herb and his helper, were fifteen of the combination desk-and-chair contraptions Leibowitz remembered from high school, each equipped with a pair of headphones.

Silence reigned, with the exception of some heavy breathing by The Oracle, then in stepped some of the hardest cases Leibowitz had ever seen, each of them garbed in prison blue. Representing every possible race and age group, the only common denominator, other than the attitude copped by all of them, was a palpable ferocity.

As the inmates eyed The Oracle, with no trace of warmth or affability, Leibowitz cringed, fearing that his notion was about to backfire.

But The Oracle, to Leibowitz's surprise, suddenly rose to the occasion.

"Make yourselves comfortable," he said in a soothing way, "as together all of us become one."

Instead of the hoots and protests Leibowitz expected, the prisoners settled docilely into their seats, with the camera rolling. Then again The Oracle spoke.

"Let us shake off our discomforts and our woes," he said, "as we, as one, take several deep, soothing, healing breaths."

To Leibowitz's dismay, the inmates did as told, following instructions far better than he could have ever dreamed possible. And when, after a prompt by The Oracle, they donned the headphones, the result was startling.

An almost magical stillness came over the room. Gone, almost miraculously, were the attitudes, the ferocity, and even any awareness of the setting.

In their place was what Leibowitz could only term a glow.

ⅩⅩⅩ

Because filming can be deceptive—a sequence that seems fantastic while being shot too often proves to be a dud when viewed in the editing room—Leibowitz was far from smug even when The Oracle praised him for his brilliance.

It was not until the prison footage was edited, then inserted into the documentary, that he allowed himself a sigh of relief, acknowledging to his editor that a potential problem had become a highlight.

But that didn't guarantee smooth sailing. As Leibowitz suspected, a call inevitably came from Herb Klein. Meekly, the emissary asked if a cut could be sent to North Carolina so that The Oracle could give his approval.

"Remember a certain conversation we had?" Leibowitz asked.

"Yes, but he'd really like to have a say."

"And I'd like to run away with a French actress named Sophie Marceau," Leibowitz replied. "But know what? Neither's happening."

)(()(

The next request, as Leibowitz suspected, came from The Oracle himself. "The prison idea was perfect!" he announced over the phone.

"And?"

"What's that mean?"

"I sense there's more coming."

"Only that I'm set to give notes when you're ready."

"What if I'm not ready?"

"Now?"

"Ever."

A strained silence ensued until at last The Oracle again spoke. "May I ask why?"

"We're planning to ask the others who appear on-screen—big names in their fields—to promote the film. Correct?

"What's that have to do with anything?"

"Editorial interference."

"I'd rather call it *input*."

"Still not happening."

"Why in hell not?"

"You've heard about never letting a camel get its nose in the tent."

"That's not very kind."

"Plus, I've got final cut."

"I can't say I'm happy."

"Your problem. Not mine."

"Are you always this way?" asked T.O.

"Actually I'm being surprisingly restrained."

With that, the conversation ended.

※※※

The Oracle's pouting, which Leibowitz heard about repeatedly thanks to calls from Herb Klein, disappeared the moment the documentary was invited to a festival in Miami.

Instantly, a public screening at The Sanctuary was requested, then scheduled. After watching the film for the first time, The Oracle hugged Leibowitz, then expressed his delight to a packed house of followers.

"I may be the master in many ways," he told the crowd. "But this man is the master of filmmaking."

Perhaps because he'd been down this kind of road before, Leibowitz couldn't help but wonder when—not *if*—the proverbial other shoe would drop.

※※※

The Oracle brought what Leibowitz thought of as his whole *tent show* to Miami. Not only did he appear on-stage, in another Hugh Hefner-style outfit, with Leibowitz for the Q&A that followed the original screening— and the one that was later added because of the demand for tickets— but he also held both an *Introductory Workshop* and what was termed a *Plenary* at another site.

Everything changed, however, when an offer to distribute the film came in from a New York-based company.

In Leibowitz's terms, The Oracle played *homing pigeon*, first requesting, then demanding, with a very contrite Herb Klein as the intermediary, that the film be re-edited in accordance with his personal wants and needs.

When Leibowitz refused, a threatening letter arrived from a North Carolina law firm. *Material breach* was invoked, together with a preposterous demand for damages.

Whereas once he would have exploded, Leibowitz simply turned the matter over to the legal staff at the Directors Guild. They, armed with the contract that Herb Klein had generated, rose instantly to their member's defense.

Simultaneously, Leibowitz's personal attorney made it clear to Herb that he was prepared to alert the Hollywood trade papers and other media that the artistic integrity of an award-winning filmmaker, despite the existence of signed documents, was being threatened by a cult-like group.

)()()(

Though *East Meets West* went on to win several honors, and Leibowitz remained in touch with several of the people who graced the screen, never again did he have even the slightest bit of contact with Herb Klein, The Oracle, or anyone of their associates.

He did, however, continue to use the meditation CD on a regular basis.

KATHARYN HOWD MACHAN

WASHING THE RICH MAN'S PORCH

Because it's muddy.
Because rain fell.
Because he had all the mulch scraped up
and hauled out of the Garden.

Because we wore shoes when we
wrote there, because his wife
gave us permission to stay dry
if rain began to fall.

Because it's his Garden now, he
bought it, the cottage, too.
Because he had a new porch
built on, right where a bright
red blossoming tree had grown
for years in memory of the woman
who killed herself right there
in the Garden, spilling blood to earth.

Because he decrees all things must be
perfect, tidy, in order, clean.

Because too much calcium has spoiled the soil,
pumped up from coral, making cement
where roots and vines once drank clear
water sprayed daily from a long hose.

Because he pays a man
every day to rake
every fallen leaf away.

Because we made a mess,
we poets and chroniclers,
helping each other
up out of the rain.

Because I led the workshop,
grateful he let me
be again in the Garden
where for sixteen years
I've shared the green vision
of the woman who turned it
from junk lot and garbage heap:
forty years of strong sane struggle.

Because he and I are both fifty-nine
and I am a woman, a poet, a teacher
without a savings account.

Because when I was sixteen
I cleaned people's toilets.
I know how to wield
a wet mop, a stiff brush.

V
LIFE . . . ART . . . LIFE . . .

JOHN MANESIS

MIRROR IMAGE

> *"Everlasting Moments" uses surfaces,*
> *texture, faces to hint at a shadow realm.*
> David Edelstein, New York Movies

Maria Larsson,
a blossoming photographer
early in the twentieth century,
learns to see her Swedish world
through a Contessa camera
she won in a lottery.

By looking through this lens,
her perspective changes
and this beleaguered housewife
marvels at unfolding scenes—

a cat perched on a sill,
icicles suspended from the eaves,
the shadow of a butterfly,
children peering through a window
at the girl who drowned herself
and was laid out in a white dress.

Near the movie's end,
she holds the camera close,
as though it were a part of her,
gazes at the looking glass
and for the first and only time
takes a picture of herself.

Does Maria see
what the camera sees,
does the camera see
what Maria sees?

CÉLINE KEATING

MY SEARCH FOR THREE PINES

Most literary pilgrimages are to where an author has lived or worked; mine involved an imaginary place.

Canada's Eastern Townships, L'Estrie, the region of Québec less than two hours south of Montreal and just over the border from Vermont, is an area rich in beauty, culture, and history. After the American Revolution, some who were loyal to the crown fled north and settled among the Québécois and the English, Scottish, and Irish settlers. From this mix come lovely juxtapositions: Both French and English are spoken here, and the towns display the sloping metal roofs of the Québécois as well as the pale rose brick homes of the Loyalists. In this rolling countryside of apple orchards, lakes, and forests, you're never far from a crisp baguette, farmhouse cheese, excellent wine, or specialty chocolate.

There is much to attract the visitor, but that's not why I talked my husband into traveling to the Townships. I was drawn by the novels of award-winning best-selling author Louise Penny, whose work is a paean to the area, and to the alluring hamlet in which she sets her mysteries. In Three Pines, homes face each other around a green jewel of a town square, the pond ices over for winter frolicking, and mysterious forests envelop all in a protective embrace. Evil comes to this world—these are murder mysteries after all—but there's always time to gather in the bistro for warm croissants and camaraderie.

I went in search of Three Pines.

Penny writes that Three Pines can only be found by those who are lost, that it does not appear on any map, but I was undaunted. Like her main character, Chief Inspector Gamache, I sniffed for clues. In *A Fatal Grace*, Penny writes of an old stone mill and an abandoned railroad station; in *The Brutal Telling*, the Riviere Bella Bella flows. An old stagecoach road, a lake, and other features are variously mentioned. But the constants were these: The village, hidden among hills and forests, occurs where four roads come together "like the spokes of a wheel" [*Still Life*]. And at one end of the commons stand three majestic pines.

We decided that we would circumnavigate the outskirts of the Townships and then spiral in, as if drawing a noose ever tighter around PennyLand, an area comprising roughly a quarter of the 5,000 square miles of the Townships. Its bull's eye was the town of Sutton, where, as I learned through her blog, the author has a home. Somewhere in PennyLand, I was convinced, would be the real town upon which Three Pines is based.

We drove over the border from upstate New York into Canada, stopping in Venice du Quebec at the head of Lake Champlain, and then headed east along a hilly road through a chain of tiny villages just skirting Vermont— Saint Armand, Abbott's Corner, Mansonville—mostly farmland rather than the woods and mountains of Penny's landscape. When we reached the eastern edge of the Townships, we headed north along the shores of sparkling Lake Memphramagog to the funky tourist town of Magog. Driving down the other side of the lake, to Ayer's Cliff and Georgeville, we came upon a stunning view of Saint-Benoit-du-Lac, the Benedictine Abbey that was the inspiration for the abbey in *The Beautiful Mystery*.

In *A Rule Against Murder*, Inspector Gamache stays at the remote Manoir Bellechase. Through careful research and clever deduction (i.e., reading the book's acknowledgements), I deduced that the model for the boutique hotel was Manoir Hovey in the town of North Hatley, where brunch surpassed even Penny's mouthwatering descriptions. As I wandered the gardens and lawns overlooking Lake Massawippi, I could feel Gamache's presence at my side, staring out at the water ringed by dark forest.

We reached bustling Cowansville on the western edge of the Townships and dined at a breakfast spot we had learned was frequented by the author, then circled in to Lac Brome (Knowlton), where I purchased a Gamache mug at the local bookshop that hosts Penny's book parties. At a cheese shop in Sutton, La Rumeur Affamée, the owner told us that there was someone in town many thought to be the model for Penny's endearing character, Olivier. The second we left the shop my husband and I turned to each other and said, "It's him!"

Sutton and Lac Brome, though quaint with shops, art galleries, B&Bs, and requisite stream and lake, respectively, were too large to be the real Three Pines. Frelighsburg, with its grassy town center, and Stanbridge East, with its beautiful old mill, felt closest in spirit, but were missing other key elements. Dunham, Lac Selby, West Brome, Sutton Junction: some were near mountains or ringed by forest, some had a covered bridge or bistro, bookstore, or a *boulangerie*. The architectural details Penny mentions were in evidence everywhere, like the loggia house style, with a balcony built on a gable wall over an open-type porch with pillars, and we even spotted a sign for the old stagecoach road. But at some point we realized that there wasn't one—not one of the dozens of villages we visited—that was formed at the juncture of several roads or that had a central commons. And few had any pines at all.

Our map was so detailed the roads looked as fragile as eyelashes. We drove every last lash until we were retracing our steps, heading down rutted dirt roads and into private driveways, making sure we hadn't overlooked a possibility. Then we learned that for a television movie made by Canadian Broadcasting Corp. of one of her books, filming had taken place in several different villages because Penny couldn't point to a prototype. After a week of travel, we headed home, frustrated and disappointed, despite having fallen in love with the area.

Of course I knew all along that Three Pines doesn't exist. Writers of fiction use snippets of the real the way birds use stray bits of grass, ribbon, or twigs to form their nests. Penny has taken the mansard roofs from one town, the old railroad station from another, the pond from yet another, and created of these elements her Shangri-La. But while the writer in me understood that, the reader, seduced by her fiction, was intent on seeking entrée to the special place that inspired her. For that's the power of fiction.

In an article on literary tourism, Sam Anderson writes, "Literature, for all its power, is an abstract transaction: A reader gives time and attention, an author gives patterns of words that call up vivid people and landscapes that— mystifyingly—are not physically there. . . . It seems like a natural human response to try to plug that gap—to look for solid, real-world corollaries for those interior landscapes. . . . It's the brain's attempt to anchor an abstraction, to make the spirit world and the boring world finally align. It is, in my experience, one of the cheapest forms of magic available."*

Once home, there was one consolation. I opened Penny's just published novel and returned to Three Pines. Once again, in some invisible space, an author and a reader's imaginations colluded to create a world.

*"The Pippiest Place on Earth" (*The New York Times Magazine*, February 12, 2012).

MICHAEL J. HESS

ANY PLACE I HANG MY HELMET

There is a place where the summer is long and the shore is longer, where a soft breeze blows in off the equator. There are no serpents or falling trees or broken cradles. There are no dreams that require interpretation. It is a place, at last, where there are chairs that will support the body for the easy hours ahead. Thoughts come together there, link. This is not the place where I live.

Where I live the summer is short and the shoreline is shorter, much of it built out of bricks and cement blocks of varied shapes and sizes. Most of the cement blocks have a grid of rebar poking out and the rebar can look like a knot of snakes that is about to strike. There are real snakes underfoot, too. Non-poisonous ones, but still. And there appears to be no place to stop, hang my helmet, sit—God, I want to sit—and craft sentences that may or may not reach readers with their messages. I am searching for that place too, stalking and staking, like a child hunting for colored eggs on the third day after the holy rise.

Then, between two trees that grow surrounded by the concrete bed, I see it. A cut of cement that might have been the corner of a foundation or a wall. The corner is flipped on its side, so that it creates a chair, where one side might support my back while the other might serve as a seat. It is perched above the real and imaginary snakes, above the horror. This corner is also wide enough—at least four feet in length—so I can put my Thermos filled with decaffeinated coffee on one side and set my backpack on the other. There are even two cement pieces situated behind this bench that can sandwich the tire of my Cannondale, serve as a makeshift parking spot.

To actively search for anything is to find oneself disappointed at times with the results, like going out and looking for a perfect shirt on the day of a big event always turns up inferior and over-priced products. A narrative where one finds exactly what one is looking for (or close to it) is almost foreign to the human experience. To experience this sequential flow is to feel the world as a kind and generous host providing everything one would want. In a good host's home, one is welcomed warmly at the door, offered a beverage (preferably wine), which is refilled without prompting. If one is staying the night, the pillows are fluffed, there is water by the bedside, and extra blankets in case one gets cold in the evening. Most important, there is a choice seat reserved at the dinner and breakfast table where one can enjoy the company and the occasion. There is care. There is concern. Get the camera ready so the picture can be snapped, the moment saved and savored for current and future generations.

Even when the dark clouds pushed across the shore later that day, no raindrops fell. The sun was merely obscured for just enough time to allow the body to cool and recharge. I do not even know how to approach the thought of a world where everything, however temporarily, turns out the way one would want it to. This is not a world I know or understand. This is some Technicolor vision rendered by geeks in dark rooms with too many pixels at their disposal. It is an unreal world. Virtual. But I cannot now deny that there are those bewildering moments when reality matches the luminosity of our dreams and our dream-makers.

The same week I found my new cement chair, I finally gave up my apartment on East 58th Street in Manhattan. I had been subleasing it since I moved to Toronto and would no longer be able to maintain that arrangement. I was twenty-seven when I moved into that apartment and forty-two when I moved out. It was an apartment rental that fell under the rent stabilization laws in New York City, the purpose of which was to provide affordable housing to individuals and families who might not have the means to live there otherwise. I was a person in New York who would not have been able to live in that neighborhood otherwise, a person who would have had to live in some far-flung enclave outside of Manhattan, using a bridge or tunnel to confirm my sentence. The apartment on East 58th Street was the first place that I could afford on my own. Prior, places needed to be subsidized, at least at times, by my parents or grandparents. There was pride in the knowledge that even if I lost my job and went bust, I would be able to scrape enough money together in order to pay the rent there. I used the mantra of those in Manhattan, mostly artists and actors, who could foresee themselves in circumstances where they might be said to be scraping by, "I could always temp."

When I filled out the forms for the apartment, I did not make enough money to qualify for the terms of the lease, namely the calculation that I needed to be making forty times the monthly rent in annual salary, so I forged my W-2s. To forge my W-2s, I photocopied the original W-2 and then used an X-Acto knife to cut out a tiny number "1" from my salary on the photocopy. This number "1" was pasted in front of my yearly salary with a glue stick on another photocopy. I then photocopied the altered document so it looked authentic. I do not remember the figure—it was low, real low, poverty-level low—but it was changed, for instance, from $20,000 to $120,000. In New York in the early nineties, an individual in his twenties used any means necessary in order to obtain an official lease in a rent-stabilized unit in the center of the city. I had no moral qualms with this act, none whatsoever.

As we moved the final materials out of the apartment on East Fifty-Eighth Street—I had left the books and bookcases, the bed and a few kitchen items for the sublessee—I discovered a box labeled college and post-college in the far back of a cabinet above the stove. I was not going to go through this box of old materials, but I could not resist opening a couple of items in order to gauge generally the contents. One letter was from my grandmother, Maxine, dated October 29, 1995. She offered me many frank words.

> *Dear Mike,*
> *I am writing to tell you why I cannot sign for the condo. If I signed and you could not make your payments, they can foreclose and take our house and farms to pay for the condo. I could not afford $800 dollar rent a month. You do not have a steady job and I am only receiving $400 a month on my social security. There is no way I can sign. We would lose all that we have and still not have a place to live. I spent $40,000 in IRA to put you through college. I have no more IRA—with the education you got you should be doing OK by now. I can send you $200 once in a while but that is the extent of what I can do anymore. Your mother is paying off your loans. Why can't you get better work than you have? Maybe you should change what you are doing and do something else. That is it as far as I am concerned.*
> *Love Grandma.*

What the grandmother might not have known is how worried the grandson was about his own future prospects. Why can't you get better work than you have? I did not know why I could not get better work than I had gotten. Maybe you should change what you are doing and do something else. Maybe I should change what I was doing and do something else. But what should that change be? The interest at the time, film and television, produced a bachelor of fine arts degree based on the completion of 128 credits of coursework. How does one arrive at another interest on the fly at a time in one's life when questions of individual identity are renting out space in every corner of the brain? I probably wanted the condo so I could have a safe place to work out those and other issues, wanted the condo so that if I lost all that I had, even myself, I would still have a safe place in which to hide out. Hide out until they found me. This was a particular time in New York when everyone I knew could see himself or herself going certifiably nuts in their studio apartments. Individuals in fetal balls wrapped in childhood blankets in a Xanax haze was the collective image of our general malaise.

There is a picture from that time in one of those boxes above the stove of a young woman in a white hospital gown in a St. Vincent's Hospital lounge. She was in this hospital for observation as one side of her body had gone mysteriously numb. "I can't feel anything there," she kept saying. The doctors poked and prodded her left side, ran blood tests, and performed the obligatory neurological exams to try to uncover this mystery. But the mystery remained. There were no adequate answers from the doctors as to why a loss of sensation in a portion of her body might have occurred, just as there were no adequate answers from the doctors as to why this cleared up one week later. "Just one of those things," I recall one person saying. Just one of those things, a string of five mono-syllabic words that could sum up many of the events of that time, a cultural credo aimed at dispossessing Generation Xers of the need for cause and effect in the events of their lives.

My grandmother died less than two years after that letter was written of an aortic aneurysm at St. Anthony's Hospital in Rockford, Illinois. "The same thing that got her mother, got her" was the narrative line the family constructed, a way we explained a world that turned on whim rather than wish. Weeks after she died, I left Chicago and moved back to New York City. I forged some federal documents, put down first and last month's rent on the place on East 58th Street, and got a job, temp to perm, that paid enough money to cover my own rent. Sometimes we need someone to die so the best parts of ourselves can shine, so we can form sentences that reach out across the human shore.

I was not going to stay in that apartment for more than a year or two at most. It was small and on a noisy street and had a college-sized refrigerator. This changed eventually, but for the first seven years in this apartment I lived with a freezer the size of two TV dinners. This is not a complaint. One can learn to live with a freezer the size of two TV dinners, just as one can learn to live with or without direct sunlight. Although there were windows in every room of this apartment, it was surrounded on all sides by taller buildings so there was only a view of the brick walls. But it worked for the reasons stated above and because it was close to Central Park. Central Park was where I would go to pen the words I was writing at the time. A home, not unlike this piece of shore at Cherry Beach with the cement chair, where my sentences might form. (I would also find sex there, and eventually my partner, but that is another story.)

My only hesitation regarding the spot along the shore at Cherry Beach was, as I've said, the real and imagined snakes. One night I went in for a little masochism and searched for information on garter snakes, which are the only type of snake on the Cherry Beach shore, on YouTube. I came upon a video that showed what is known as a snake-mating ball. A snake-mating ball occurs when a female red-striped garter snake releases a pheromone as she awakens from hibernation. It signals all the males in the vicinity to come over and pile on top of her. The snakes, circumscribed as such, form the shape of a ball. The snake-mating ball concludes when one of the snakes penetrates the single red-striped female with one of his penises. There are two, in case one breaks off. Most snake mating balls involve twenty to twenty-five red-striped garter snakes. At the Narcisse Snake Dens, in Manitoba, however, there can be tens of thousands slithering in often overlapping balls in a series of pits. This serpentine Caligula draws many visitors in the early spring. Andrew and I plan to visit these caves next year. To see one snake in the wild is to jump, but to see thousands is to be confronted with a species dead set on survival by any means necessary. It is to simultaneously stand in the primal space where our deepest fears and fascinations reside.

E.O. Wilson in *In Search of Nature* explains that our fear and fascination of snakes is due to "their ability to remain hidden, the power of their sinuous limbless bodies, and the threat from venom injected hypodermically through sharp hallow teeth." Wilson would go on to hypothesize that we are predisposed to fear these creatures because they were—and in many parts of the world, are—a threat to human survival. But one might question his logic here: do we actually have to be biologically prepared to jump when a body with no arms or legs and a mouth full of fangs that acts like hypodermic needles crawls out from a hiding space?

On this particular shore, snakes are not the only species that strike automatic and evolutionary fear in the minds of many people. There are also arachnids crawling and hopping on every surface in sight. On a branch behind me is a black and yellow-striped spider that looks like it came out of a Dr. Seuss book. Perhaps it will open its mouth and recite a rhyme that might pull me back to a self that does not think in terms of fetal and serpentine balls and permanent homes. Many of the spiders are small, say the size of an adult's pinky fingernail, and come in basic black and gray. These spiders not only creep and crawl, but jump with the combustive energy of popping corn. There are other spiders, almost microscopic, that can be seen, because they are scarlet red, zigzagging over all of the cement blocks. Wipe one with a finger and there is a trail of red that cuts across the surface. These almost microscopic creatures are some form of mite, either red spider mites or clover mites. They seem to move without thought, a random jutting to and fro, like electrons searching out possible paths inside the nuclei of atoms. I might set up a camera with a telephoto lens and record their activity. In the edit room, I could then slow the tape down to see if there are any patterns to the movements of these mites.

A little research shows that at least some of the movements of these mites are not random. Clover mites look for a location with lots of sunshine in order to lay their eggs and the high crevices in the cement slabs at Cherry Beach make an ideal spot; the crevices also protect the eggs from predators and environmental factors. Once these eggs hatch, the larvae travel down to the grasses or clover to feed. Then they travel back up to the protected crevices when they want to shed their skin. At certain times of the year, clover mites at all stages can be moving on these surfaces in all directions in order to achieve their developmental ends; hence, red bugs bounding on every available surface.

There are even red bugs on the two poplar trees that are growing through the cement shore at my new writing space. Because of the way they are situated, these poplars provide a vertical frame for the vista of lake and sky. The roots of the poplar contain shoots, called suckers, which enable the tree to create clones of itself. Each sucker that arises from the roots contains identical genetic information as the parent plant. I bring up the suckers because these two trees before me may contain the same genetic information: the sides of the natural frame may be identical. That objects so alike should be allowed to exist in nature forces us to construct an idea of identity where all living things may not be unique. And if identity is not necessarily unique, then what is it? Who or what are we?

There is female poplar a little to the west (poplars reproduce by pollination when they are not reproducing by sucker output), which has dangling seeds, called catkins, that resemble the long articulated earrings that women wore in the seventies. From late May through June these seeds burst open and scatter a white cottonseed that blows in the wind and lands on every surface in the kingdom. Tufts of white seed on every leaf, blade and burr, the world can look like it has been decked out for Halloween with bags of synthetic spider web.

On the day I first viewed this particular tree, the sun was dropping behind it, which highlighted the seeds, not falling down, but blowing upward, making the scene look like a reverse snowfall in June. The world at that moment seemed unhinged, a snow globe temporarily flipped by some benevolent hand in order to see the white flakes circulate. There was an urge to grab onto something to secure my position. Trees, the strongest, the most rooted and solid structure on the planet, seemed the only hope at that moment. If I could hold onto one to keep my bearings, I thought, I might survive this strange new world. Of course, it might be more fun to let myself go, see myself spin in a direction unknown, land in some new place where I might declare residency.

There is nothing truly strange about an upward current of wind. In New York, one sees a plastic garbage bag or another piece of trash caught in a convection of wind, pushing it toward the sky all the time. To sit in a skyscraper or a studio in Manhattan and see the windblown objects out the window is to appreciate the poetry of debris in the wind. It can pull one away from the computer screen, the work or life task, and temporarily halt those processes that help make the economy and our lives run. To this end, looking out the window in an urban environment is unproductive and therefore anti-economic. There may come a day when the windows in all the buildings are replaced with concrete, so one can forget all together the wonders and terrors the real world offers.

I suppose I prefer my world with a little mess, even if it is in the form of circulating trash, or the reproductive droppings of a certain female tree. According to *The Oxford Encyclopedia of Trees of the World*, "male [poplar] trees are preferred in public spaces" to female ones because the fruit of the female tree makes such a mess and requires city and private resources to keep the streets and the yards clean. Well, male trees are preferred if one does not like the look of cottonseed floating through the air and piling up like snow. Male trees are preferred if one is not too into the poetics of trees, if one would not mind a cement wall to a window. If one, at last, would wish to impress on the landscape a tree of a singular gender.

On the rocks in front of me at the new writing space are four pools of paint the color of Easter—Pepto-Bismol pink, olive green, lemon yellow, and robin's-egg blue. I say pools of paint because when the sun is bright and the temperature warm, the paint liquefies and people can dip their fingers into the different colors and let their imaginations go wild. How did the paint get here? Perhaps some artist came out to interpret the vista and forgot her palette, so she used the rocks to arrange her colors. Or, perhaps a child came out here and decided to pour, instead of spread, her paint. Interestingly, the paint has even trapped some of the red clover mites. One wonders how many bug bodies, how much red, would it take for the four pools of color to noticeably change hue? I like the thought of paint made with bug meat and bug blood.

Stand on the blocks with the paint and one can see, to the East, a swing fashioned to a tree with a bungee cord. The tree that this swing hangs on is an old tree, and it, like the poplar, can hold its own against the cement at its skirt. On my most recent visit, a saxophonist was sitting near the swing playing by improvisation. The tune he was playing came in on the wind. Like the music emitting from Jay Gatsby's home in West Egg, I thought alternately of the promise of a party that might never end and of a party that would definitely end. I then thought back to a dream I had the night prior about a party I attended with writing team Joan Didion and John Gregory Dunne.

John, Joan, and I were in a living room with green Berber carpet and pale green walls. It looked like a room from the time when I was a child in the seventies. There were a lot of people in this living room. John and Joan handed me a book that they had inscribed. The inscription read, in pencil, "Great meeting you at People Like Us. Love, John and Joan." The signatures were unrecognizable. The three of us then had our arms looped around each other as we stood in a close circle with our heads touching, a holy triad of writers conferring secrets of the trade. Next, Joan and I danced around a glass coffee table. There were clear drinks in our hands and there was lots of laughter. She was not the older Joan who wrote *The Year of Magical Thinking* and *Blue Nights*, but the young Joan who would finish *The White Album* and *Slouching Toward Bethlehem*, among others, in a room in her parent's house in Sacramento, the one with long hair and bare feet and those sentences. Then, Joan was lighting a cigarette and getting into a fight with John. This dream, like every party, ended on its particular note, and left a residue on the subject, a gauzy trail of image and sound.

I am not going to offer an interpretation of this dream because dream interpretation has fallen out of fashion in the popular culture. When was the last time someone stood around a water cooler or refrigerator filled with Poland Spring water bottles discussing dreams and dreamscapes? Dream interpretation fell out of fashion because the debate over whether dreams have meaning or do not have meaning never came to any decisive conclusion. Psychoanalysts and psychologists have been little help in the matter, when they offer that there can be many interpretations of a single dream and that those interpretations can change through time as the client changes. To allow multiple interpretations and then to allow interpretations on top of interpretations throughout time sounds like hogwash to most people, a way for the mental arts to sidestep the need for at least a little accuracy. There was even a feeling that one could make the case for any interpretation if it felt true and, if anything could turn out to be true based on feeling, then the point of the dream seemed to come down to contractual terms, where things were agreed upon based on the push and pull of two adversaries (analyst and analysand) who pretended to be teammates.

I do, in fact, believe that dreams have meaning, just as I believe in an unconscious that is the fontal bedrock from which all desire springs. I just do not necessarily believe that the dream or the unconscious can be fully unearthed, or even understood. Regarding my dream of Joan and John, I will only say that it felt mighty nice to have the four arms of two literary giants surround me for one night, even if it was only in a dream.

The swing that hangs on the old tree by the shore is not a dream. Who could see a real swing on a shore and not have the urge to hop on its seat and drift back and forth? To swing back and forth must be to recall the first moments of life in the arms of the ones who loved us. It must be to stop the internal crack and buzz of contemporary living and fall into a narcotic haze where nothing is of consequence, but everything is all right. That brief moment when everything is all right. That too brief moment when everything is all right. It soon stops being all right. The serpent enters the shore or the dream. Early family dramas declare war on the present. The trees are downed, not considered. The author alerts the reader to natural or evil forces on the horizon.

I am reminded of the childhood verse:

Hush-a-bye baby
On the tree top,
When the wind blows
The cradle will rock.
When the bough breaks,
The cradle will fall,
And down will fall baby
Cradle and all.

This verse encapsulates quite nicely the world as I understand it. It describes a world where everything does not, in fact, turn out all right. A world where the hosts, whether human or animal or supernatural, are not always kind and generous. A world where the blanket is pulled off at the moment when one needs its warmth the most. A world where we close our eyes and encounter scenes and flash images that we can only pretend to decipher. A world where we put our children to sleep on the tops of trees, where we wait for the wind to blow, the bough to break, and the baby to course through the air. What happens to that child? What happens to us all? I have actually grown quite comfortable with this world, reconciled myself to the horror and beauty that lurks under the surfaces and in the interiors of all the places that I inhabit. I am so comfortable with this world that I did not flinch when the black flies hatched a few weeks later and infested my new writing space with their glorious buzz and bite.

CARL PALMER

TOOLS

When I'm unable to get the lid off
a jar of dill pickles, Dad hands me
the same bent butter knife he used
earlier to pry open his car key ring.

A toolbox tray in the utility room
has a few rusted nails, some wire,
two hacksaw blades, an ink pen,
several sockets and a toothbrush.

There's a pair of vise grip pliers,
three flat tips and a cross point in
the kitchen drawers I've seen while
searching for a roll of scotch tape.

Dad had tools in the barn, car trunk
and well house he could never find,
that one of us kids must have used
and didn't put back where they belonged.

I arrive to borrow a hammer from my
brother's organized garage filled with
tools for every job to find him scraping
mud from his shoe with a butter knife.

JOHN SIBLEY WILLIAMS

REPURPOSING

A smooth metal cartridge,
cooled in disuse,
is plucked by an orphan
from a mass grave of unfired things
and redefined around her neck
as a temporary charm
to ward off the tide.

She stands on the other side
of a tiny malformed ocean,
tracing someone's name in the sand
with her toes.
I see her fingering the trinket
as she looks over the world
and straight through me,

as again she feels the waters
swallowing her ankles,
rising over a city
that drowned long ago,
as again things disentomb and reignite and discharge,
as the dead alive within her
pursue what they'd forgotten to consume.

RUTH MARGOLIN SILIN

THE ILLEGAL

He can wait for a moonless night
when border watchers doze and
lose count of their daily catch.
He can stay, leaning against
the wall of the *casita*, sipping his mezcal,
letting it slide slowly down his throat,
his thirst unquenched.
He can spend his days
watching clouds drift over the divide,
looking like the angels his mother
prays to.
He thinks about his mother's
prayers, his father's voice repeating
cuida a tu madre.
He thinks about staying while the mirror
shows his hair turned white, his dreams
empty as the bottles surrounding him.

He hears what José and Juan and
Juan's brother Miguel told him, that
somewhere on the other side a lady waits
with up-stretched arms and lighted torch.

He runs.

MARY KAY RUMMEL

BAPTIST
for Tim

Drenched in sweetness, I feed hummingbirds,
paint monarchs on the backs of turtles.
Suddenly your cry—a spear in my side!
I stroke your scars, counting and naming
the dry seas, the craters and plains.
You are buckskin in patches, salty, speckled like a sky.
Afterward I wash you in the muddy Mississippi,
release your sins to live with the carp
hiding in their church of reeds.
I wrap a silk shirt over your thin, grieving shoulders.
Your eyes—wheel shafts of aquamarine.

But I warn you, my heretic, the sun is ruled by darkness.
Kingfisher stalks the day, dive bombing from his perch
in tall cottonwood, scattering little fish in his wake.
We live in wildness where that blue torpedo
means no harm and prey adores the perfect dive.
You are my blue beloved slipping
into narrow shadows that separate
dragonflies from cruel burning acacia.

LAURENCE SNYDAL

LEONARDO'S HEART

*"How could you describe this heart in words
without filling a whole book?"*

Da Vinci, 1513

Da Vinci drew a knife where blood once ran
Through living flesh, flaying and laying bare
Ligatured levers, secret sockets, where
He found the architecture of a man.
Muscle and sinew, bone and brain exposed
By his blade found their way to brush and art,
Discovered. So all could now see how heart
And artery and thew and thought disposed
Themselves. More than that, of course, he designed
Fortresses and how to breach their walls, wings,
Parachutes, armor, clever everythings
That others hadn't thought to think or find.

He drew and painted all who'd pay his wage.
But he himself didn't pay bills. He praised
Those he must please, distrusted most, and phrased
Clever reflections on a journal's page.

Here was a man who took a world apart,
Whose body's book could barely hold his heart.

VIDA CROSS

THE GREAT MIGRATION

Daddy said
at seventeen
he ran
from the white racist police of Mississippi
because he'd stole a chicken

He grabbed his thirteen-year-old wife
and high tailed it north to Chicago

This was the love story we were told

When he died
his Mississippi daughter showed

Sat with us side by side

TYREE DESHAWN WILSON

DREAM COLLAPSING

A taste of the future picture me no boundaries king, I never thought I'd make it this far. Just remember I'm dreaming, future me, picture me, untouchable man amazing, the last one left in a world of very few . . . The way they look at me and say king, got me leaning and teary eyed because I'm dreaming. Reality got me shook because it's real. . . . It ain't hard to tell.

HUMAN

Be happy about what they say when they be dissin, because you are blessed with your affliction. What defines beauty? and what is flesh? How beautiful is a man or a woman if you flip them inside-out? Or how intelligent is a man if his brains are blown out? Really who do you think you are?

INSOMNIA

At night as I lay upon my bed I know the world is still awake; I can't sleep, not knowing keeps my mind tormented. I mean how can a blind man sleep?! I'm told life is hard you gotta play it safe, but I'm also told life is too short. . . . I know these thoughts are vain, I know life tomorrow is not promised. In which way will I be slain? I'm going insane because until that day I must slave in one way or another.

PRISONER TO LOVE

Beautiful woman of my dreams, why do you torment me? Your eyes slay my heart, and my day is ruined at even the thought of wronging you in any way. Brief encounters in dreams have been our meeting place, but in this life you must exist! But alas I am very far from perfect. Who am I to imprison you in my thoughts?

SLEEP

Last night I lay in bed, woke listening as my clock spoke, it giving me insight about time and asking about life and my approach. It named all the greats time bred and gave me the number of ticks before they croaked. I couldn't sleep, because all night it just spoke and spoke and spoke. Terrified from the reality it revealed I didn't dare let my eyes close. I learned that the average U.S life span is only give or take eighty years or so. It told me the penalty of laziness was like running a race for no gold. Because even if I don't live I still got to live, because I still got to eat. There's too much work to be done in this short life, there's no time to spend a third of it sleep.

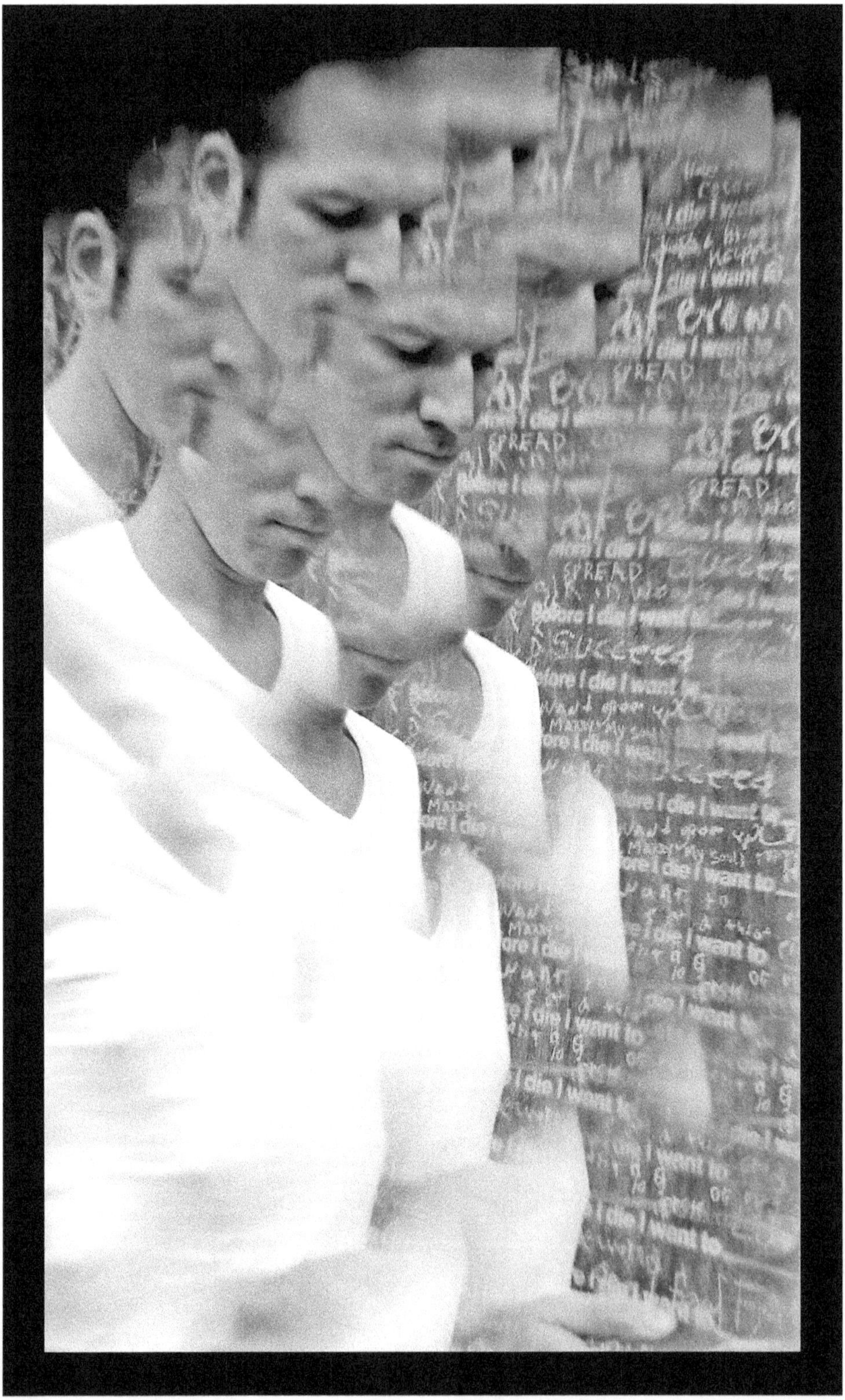

MICHAEL ONOFREY

KLIMT

At the far end of the room there was a piano with a folded American flag on top of it. Nearby, a window cast rays of light that slanted downward. The piano was black and shiny, the flag a fat triangle. The window was large and small-paned with an arch at the top. He'd have to paint those frames one at a time with a one-and-a-half-inch angled brush if she were to hire him to paint the living room. But it wasn't only the living room she wanted a price for. There was a bedroom as well.

"Yes," she said. "This is the living room. The bedroom is this way."

She led him down a carpeted hall. They came to the last door, the third door. She opened it and they went in. It was a girl's room, but things had been removed. Clothes, stuffed animals, photographs, posters and such were missing. The curtains and the wallpaper and the smell, though, told the story.

He was in whites, painter's whites. It was a warm day, middle of November. He had a clipboard in hand. The woman's name, Marilyn Baskin, along with a phone number and an address were at the top of a blank sheet of paper on the clipboard.

"You want this room painted, not papered."

"Yes."

"Okay. Let me tweak the wallpaper down at the baseboard here to see how many layers of paper there are."

"Sure."

He took a putty knife from a narrow pocket along the side of his pants and got down on a knee and lifted a wedge of paper from the wall.

"Two layers," he said.

"Is that bad?"

"Not bad, not good. I'm just calculating time. Four layers would take more time to remove."

She nodded. He stood up.

"Can't you paint over the wallpaper?"

"No."

A pair of windows looked out on a backyard, and in that yard an elm was shedding brown leaves.

"The curtains have to come down and the bookcases and furniture moved," Wayne said. "In this room and the living room. Do you want me to do it, or do you want to do it? If I do it, I'll charge you. It'll go into the price."

"Oh, I hadn't thought of that."

"A lot of people don't. That's why I mention it."

"Well, I guess I want you to do it."

"Okay."

"But I'll take the books off the shelves and pack them in boxes."

She meant the books in the living room because the bookcases in the bedroom were empty.

"That'll help a lot," he said, "and if you could put the boxes in another room that would help too."

"Okay. I'll do that."

"There are paintings on the walls in the living room. Do you want to take them down and put them someplace?"

"Yes. I'll do that too."

"Okay. And do you want those paintings to go back to where they are now, you know, on the same hooks?"

"Yes."

"Then I'll leave the hooks."

"But I don't want the curtains to go back up. I'm going to throw them away. I want to put up mini-blinds in this room and the living room."

"Okay. I'll remove the brackets and patch the holes."

"And I'd like you to this between the middle of December, December seventeenth, and January tenth. Can you do it then?"

He thought a moment and then said, "Yes."

She looked at him. He was a rangy man with thinning russet hair combed straight back. He wore bifocals and so did she, but her glasses didn't have a horizontal line between top and bottom prescriptions as did his.

"Do you want the inside of that closet painted?" He pointed.

"Yes."

He opened the closet door and looked in. It was a walk-in closet and it was empty except for two cardboard boxes on the floor. There was a light. He turned it on and got out a tape measure and measured the length and width and height of the closet. He wrote those figures down and turned the light off and closed the door.

He handed her a color chart, and while she looked at it he measured the bedroom. It was larger than usual, but this didn't surprise him. Unlike most of the houses in the Valley, which were tract homes, many of the houses in this area, Studio City, were custom built.

They returned to the living room and he measured that room. She stood and watched him, jeans on her legs, a gray sweatshirt with the sleeves cut off at mid-forearm on her torso. She was very thin. Her eyes were hazel and her hair was dark brown, and her hair was close-cropped to where it hugged her skull. She wore very little make up.

On the mantle of the fireplace there was a menorah. The mantle was painted white. Wayne asked if she wanted the mantle repainted that same white or if she wanted it a different color. She said she didn't care. Wayne said he'd paint it the same color as the other woodwork, a semi-gloss soft gray, the color she had selected minutes before while they were in the bedroom—both rooms a light gray, woodwork semi-gloss, walls flat. Wayne got out a pocket calculator and did the math. After he finished, he stood a moment and then wrote a figure down and told her what it was. She said, "Fine."

Wayne looked at the folded triangular flag that was on top of the piano. His eyes had gone there a number of times, and now they went there again.

"It's what you think it is," she said.

"I've seen them on TV and in the movies."

"So had I, and now I have one in my house."

Wayne shifted his weight. It was a quiet house, a settled house, a clean house. No tobacco. The living room and the bedroom didn't need painting. In the living room it was only that she was going from Navajo White, an off-white with a brown tint, to City Lights, another off-white but with a gray tint. In the bedroom it was a flower-patterned wallpaper she was erasing.

"I'm sorry," Wayne said.

She stuck a hand in the pocket of her jeans, thumb left out and hooked over the seam.

"You'd think I'd have put that flag away by now instead of leaving it there," she said.

She took her hand out of the pocket and brought it toward her face but stopped. She lowered the hand to where it hung at her side like her other hand. She wore no jewelry of any sort, not even a wristwatch.

"I'm going to walk down the street to that Starbucks on the corner," Wayne said. "Do you want to go down there and have a cup of coffee?"

She looked at him. He brought a hand up and adjusted his bifocals. He was clean-shaven. Tiredness described his long face.

"Okay. Let me get my bag."

She turned and left the room, which left Wayne alone to look around and to think. He had no idea why he had invited her down the street for coffee. It just came out of his mouth as if on its own.

Framed photos, mostly black-and-white, pottery, mostly Native American, cast metal, mostly Hindu or Buddhist, were on the walls and surfaces throughout the room. Wayne's eyes stopped at a picture of a woman who was dressed in black and who was sitting on a bench. Next to the woman there was another woman who was in a ballet costume. The woman in black was middle-aged, the woman in the ballet costume young. The young woman, the ballerina, was bent over and was looking at her ankle that she was grasping with one hand. The middle-aged woman held a black umbrella at a downward slant, umbrella collapsed. The middle-aged woman's eyes couldn't be seen, but her nose and mouth could. A black hat was on her head, rim of the hat covering her eyes. The hat looked stiff. The ballet dancer's face couldn't be seen at all because she was too bent over, her face too much at downward angle. Her hair was in a bun.

"Degas," Marilyn said. She had walked up to beside him and he hadn't heard her. The living room was carpeted.

"There's something about it," Wayne said.

"Yes, there is."

"It's a nice painting."

"Actually, it's pastel on paper, but of course this is only a print. The original is at the new Getty."

"What's it called?"

"*Waiting.*"

"*Waiting*?"

"Yes. They are waiting to audition. Well, the ballerina is waiting to audition."

"Really?"

"Yes. Why?"

"I thought the ballerina was done. She looks tired, and the older woman looks disappointed, or weary."

Marilyn put a hand under her chin while she looked at the framed print. Her other hand held a cloth bag. "Yes," she said, "but then why is it titled, *Waiting*?"

"Maybe they're waiting for the results. Or maybe they already know the results, but they have to wait anyway."

XOXOX

People were on the sidewalk. Traffic was on Ventura Boulevard. They sat at a round table at the edge of the sidewalk, windows of Starbucks at their backs. The day's warmth lingered, but something in the air suggested a sweater. Marilyn had put on a sweater, a bone-colored knit. Wayne had taken a sweatshirt from the cab of his pickup truck and had put that on. It was four-thirty in the afternoon.

"I've never been here before," Marilyn said. "I live just up the block, and I've never been to this Starbucks. Others, yes, but never this one. I think it's because it's so close."

"I like watching people," Wayne said. "Faces, hairdos, tattoos, shopping bags, clothes, conversations. I like eavesdropping. I come here often."

"Do you live nearby?"

"No, not really."

Marilyn sipped her coffee, coffee latte. Wayne sipped his coffee, coffee latte.

"But I often work around here, but even when I'm not working here, I drive over and have coffee—people walking, people talking, people shopping. It alleviates my situation."

"What's your situation?" Marilyn asked.

"I live alone, I work alone. I like it that way, but I need this."

They sipped their coffees.

"I went to the desert," Marilyn said. "I found it near Pearblossom, off some dirt roads that went to the foothills, near a place called Llano. I walked, and I felt the heat, felt the dryness, felt the grit beneath my shoes. I needed to feel something, something on my face, something on my arms, something under my feet. I still do. I still go out there." She paused, and then said, "But now it's changed. The season's changed and the air's changed and the no-nothing plants have changed. I see doves. Last week I saw three coyotes."

They sat, facing the sidewalk and the street while looking at one another with a sideways view, one elbow on the table, Marilyn's left elbow, Wayne's right.

"You went to the desert when you got the flag."

"After."

Wayne nodded.

"After the forms, insurance, and bureaucracy. After the ceremony."

Wayne was looking at her and listening.

"After the condolences, after the sympathy, after the advice, and after the food that was piled on the tables and the counters and jammed into the refrigerator." She paused. "After I threw the food away."

Wayne lifted his cup and sipped his coffee.

"Someone told me, 'All Americans grieve for your daughter.'"

"You don't believe it."

"No."

Marilyn raised her cup and sipped her coffee. Her lips were thin.

"These people are not grieving," she said, and indicated the people passing on the sidewalk.

"How do you know?"

"Because I was like them."

Wayne nodded.

"I'm not angry. I wish I was still like them."

Marilyn sipped her coffee.

"I walk in the desert—I sweat, I hear my breath, I hear my shoes on the dirt. I feel something on my skin."

"Husband, father?"

"He never existed. I had lovers. I got pregnant. I wanted the child. I didn't want the husband."

"The house indicates that."

"Indicates what?"

"Indicates no man."

"You see houses. You know."

"I don't know. I guess."

"People told me to be political, to be religious, to be patriotic."

Marilyn raised her cup and sipped her coffee. Wayne sipped his coffee.

"There's something over there," Marilyn said.

Wayne looked.

Across the street people were waiting for the signal to change.

"The man with the red cap," Marilyn said.

The light changed and the crowd came off the curb.

"George."

"George? What's on his shoulder?" Marilyn asked.

"Momoko."

"Momoko?"

"George's pet monkey."

"Oh."

"Momo is Japanese for peach. Ko is often part of a girl's name. It's tacked on at the end—Yoko, Keiko, Hanako. Ko carries the meaning of girl or child or young woman. Some girls in Japan are named Momoko. This is what George told me."

"I see."

"But George's monkey, Momoko, is male."

The crowd reached the sidewalk and parted. George, a plump man with smooth cheeks on a round face, joined those going left, which put him on a course in front of Starbucks.

"Well, well, well," said George, having stopped and smiled. The monkey, about the size of a cantaloupe, was looking right and left, and up and down.

"Hello, George. How are you?"

"Fine, thank you. Well, mostly fine."

"George, this is Marilyn. Marilyn, this is George."

"How do you do, Marilyn?"

"How do you do?"

"Well, as I just said, mostly fine, but there are bugs. I mean, we are never completely correct, are we?" George grinned.

"This is Momoko. Momoko, take a bow." George raised a hand and extended an index finger. The monkey, in a blue skirt, had a tiny yellow hat on its head. Glancing at George's finger, Momoko bowed quickly. Marilyn chuckled. George said, "He's such a ham." George renewed his grin.

Momoko's reconnaissance found a leashed dog, a very large dog, coming along the sidewalk. Momoko went into a crouch and cowered behind George's neck. As the dog went by, Momoko inched around George's neck to hide from the dog.

"Wayne, I was going to call you."

"Oh?"

"That mural that you helped me with."

"Which one?"

"The one in my house."

"Yes."

"It has to come down, piece by piece, taken apart, and then transported to Pacific Palisades where it needs to be put back up in a house over there."

"You're kidding."

"A gentleman, an acquaintance of Benny's, bought it. Benny came over and took some pictures, and Dale, the man in Palisades, saw the pictures and wanted to come over for a look-see. After he saw it, he just had to have it."

"I'm busy until sometime in January."

"Perfect. I don't want it to come down before the holidays."

"Okay. I'll give you a call after the first of the year."

George smiled, gapped teeth in a wide mouth.

"Well, Momoko and I have got to scoot—errands, shopping, what have you." George gestured toward down the street.

"Nice meeting you, Marilyn. Be talking to you, Wayne."

George walked away, Momoko looking backwards and forwards, brown eyes blinking like a couple of shutters.

"A mural?" Marilyn said.

"Plywood cut into shapes. Not construction-grade plywood, but plywood with a hardwood veneer, a smooth surface to paint on. The pieces are mounted on a wall in this alcove-like room off of George's living room. The way it's set up, the mural looks like it's framed if you look at it from the living room, which is where you have to look at it from. I had no idea how to bid on the job, so I told him he'd have to pay me by the hour. Money isn't an issue with George. It's just that he's extremely particular."

Marilyn nodded.

"It's a picture of Hanuman, a Hindu deity, half monkey, half man. George's Hanuman has three heads, and each one has a different expression. Because he used pieces of painted plywood cut into shapes, which I cut, sanded and shaped under his tutelage, he was able to create a 3-D sort of image, or images. The pieces of the plywood are elevated off the wall at varying distances, often overlapping, so that if you take a couple of steps right or left the images change. Hanuman is actually pieces. It's not one whole thing. But when you look at it, it's whole. Your eye puts it together no matter from where you view it, and it changes depending on angle."

"Really?"

"I bet he sold that mural for a lot of money."

"I'd like to see it."

"I'm sure George wouldn't mind if you took a look at it before it comes down. After I call him, I'll call you."

"It's a date."

Wayne sipped his coffee. Marilyn sipped her coffee.

"But let me warn you, George is very hospitable. He likes to sit people down with a cup of coffee and a piece of cake and detail his problems—Momoko, Benny, Larry, asthma, hay fever, the email he got from his sister last week who lives in Reno."

"Does he ever talk about art?"

"Not with me he doesn't. But of course I'm only a pair of hands, but that doesn't exempt me from gossip, complaints, and bitchery."

Marilyn smiled.

"We go to the paint store. He's got these swatches of color. All his colors are custom colors. I stand while George deals with the counter person. My only input is quantity. He works for the studios sometimes. Set design, if I'm not mistaken."

"What do you think I do?"

"If you go down Ventura Boulevard, here, to the Crippled Elephant, you can see one of George's creations. I helped him with that one too. In there, it's Ganesh, half elephant, half man."

"What do you think I do?"

"Benny, the man he mentioned, runs the Crippled Elephant. It's his place. It's a bar—tables, booths, shuffleboard, Wurlitzer jukebox, pinball machine. Benny has a cat, a Siamese, which is usually perched on the bar. The cat's name is Raymond. You should see Raymond and Momoko eyeball each other."

"What do you think I do?"

"Have you been there—the Crippled Elephant?"

"No."

"Well, in that case, I'd say that you're not gay, because if you were, you'd have probably popped in there."

"Are you gay?"

"No."

"What do you think I do?"

"I don't know what you do. What do you do?"

"Guess. You've been in my house."

"No heavy lifting."

Marilyn chuckled.

Wayne brought his cup up and sipped, Marilyn looking at his hand, the hand that held the paper cup—skin dry, fingers long, veins raised. Marilyn said, "How old are you?"

"Fifty-nine."

"Fifty-nine?"

"Soon to be sixty. Come on retirement. The sooner the better. Although I doubt if it'll ever arrive. I got a feeling I'm going to have to keep on working until . . . until forever."

"I'm forty-five. I thought you were my age."

Wayne sipped his coffee. His eyes were gray.

"I teach art at a college. But I paint. I have a studio at home. It's in the detached garage that's in the backyard. Mostly watercolors. Now and then I have a show."

"Should I know your name?"

"You already do."

"Yes, I guess I do."

"Do you have any flaws, any . . . ?"

"You mean Viagra?"

Marilyn looked at him and saw a crooked smile. She threw her head back and laughed. Her neck was skinny. Her Adam's apple showed.

"It's been a long time," she said.

"I've never tried it, but I think I might like to give it a go just to see if it enhances the experience."

"I mean the back and forth."

"The flirting?"

"Yes."

They picked up their cups and sipped.

"Have you ever walked in the desert?" Marilyn asked.

"I lived in the desert. One time for six months, the second time for three months. The Negev, Israel, a kibbutz. I was young."

"Israel?"

"Yes."

"I told my daughter to go there. I told her to go to a kibbutz. She wanted adventure, she wanted excitement, she wanted something to do. I told her to go to a kibbutz, I told her to go to India, I told her to go to New Mexico."

"I've been to India. Twice."

"She was in college. She was restless, she was full of energy, she wanted something to do. 'Something real,' was what she said."

"India is unreal."

"'Something real'—and now I have a flag on my piano."

"Do you play the piano?"

"Not anymore."

"When are you going to put the flag away?"

ЖОЖОЖ

They walked on a vacant sidewalk, lawns and parkways neatly trimmed. It was dark, but there were streetlights and lights through windows.

"Do you like sushi?" Marilyn asked.

"Yes."

"Do you drink beer?"

"Yes."

"I feel like beer and sushi tonight. Do you feel like that?"

"I'll drive home and shower and change."

"There's a place within walking distance."

"I'll return in a cab. I don't drink and drive anymore."

"I'll follow you and bring you back. We can walk from my house. Where do you live?"

"Sun Valley. It's not that far away, but . . . it's different than Studio City."

"Have you seen Klimt's work?"

"I don't know."

"I have a book with some nice plates. I'll show you his work."

"I'd like to see it."

MILT MONTAGUE

THANKSGIVING NIGHT

we both were tired from a long day of traveling
at last we were home and entered our building
Evelyn stopped to chat with the doorman
I forged ahead to the elevator bank
as I turned to call her my almost 90 year old body
lost it's balance on the polished terrazzo floor
there I was, arms flailing about clawing at the air
trying to grab on to something . . . anything

i knew i was going down

everything was happening in slow motion
my desperate attempt to break my fall
I knew that I might break a hip . . .
tragic at my age . . .
awareness that I was falling
there was nothing to stop me
except the cold stone floor
that rose up to meet me

we met hard
the momentum carried my head forward
to meet the implacable stone
face down

i was fully conscious, thank god,
my wife Evelyn and the doorman, Wayne,
dashed over to help me

are you okay? . . . i think so

anything broken . . .
any pain ? . . . nnnnoooo
you're bleeding from your left eyebrow

I'm . . . O . . . K
no pain . . . so I guess . . . nothing is broken
help me . . . sit up . . . against that pillar
i've got some tissues in my pocket

Wayne suggested calling 911
I hesitated while pressing the tissues
against my eyebrow
Evelyn ran upstairs to our apartment
got a cold compress to staunch the bleeding

pressure on the wound helped
but the profuse bleeding would not stop
we discussed the possibility of concussion
maybe we should call 911
still bleeding . . . a lot
what the hell . . . Wayne . . . please call 911
in less than ten minutes screaming sirens
announced an ambulance with two young men
gently inquiring as to what happened
and which hospital we preferred

my cardiologist and nephrologist are at Weill-Cornell
soon we were on our way there
at 1:00 a.m. the streets were deserted
didn't realize they were so bumpy
medics were extremely caring and attentive
Dave Eli held the compress against my head
gently but firmly all the way to the hospital

welcomed most cordially by a male nurse
attending doctor very reassuring as she evaluates
the damage and orders a cat scan of my head

in a few minutes I am wheeled up to radiology
no waiting and shortly back to emergency room
results of scan excellent as my md consults
with the chief physician on whether
the wound can be glued

i thought they were joking
they were not
and at 3:30 a.m.
the gash was glued together
at 4:30 a.m. we left for home via a taxi
that was waiting at the discharge exit

by 5:00 a.m. we arrived home safe and sound
with one glued eyebrow, one swollen cheek,
and a helluva black eye

god bless Evelyn, Wayne, 911, the emergency room,
male nurses, lady doctors and Michael Bloomberg

FRANK SALVIDIO

"WORDS, WORDS, WORDS . . ."

"In the beginning was the word": because
My sister taught me how to read when I
Was four, my life without a stop or pause
Proceeds as from that day. No time's gone by,
It seems, since then: no thing—no thought—is real
Until it's said by me; no tenet's held
Until I've fashioned words that will reveal
Its perspicacity—the truth I've spelled
Into new sounds that hover in the air.
Nor have I any feelings, then, unless
My voice expresses them in verse somewhere—
In poem, lay, or song: unless I bless
Them into living sound, they cannot be,
As till I lived in words, there was no me.

WIT

Said words, like bullets, cannot be recalled:
It is too late already, though we rue
Them in their breath, and are abashed—appalled—
To see at once the fatal harm they do,
That end a lifetime's friendship in a trice,
Or strike a blameless, unintended mark,
And turn a gift for punning to a vice
Of laughter, making what was lightsome dark.
Why do we do it—we who have the gift
For words we can't control, who shoot them forth
As from a scatter gun? A tongue too swift,
A brain too slow to muzzle it, or both:
There is more harm than good in sudden wit,
But I have been too late in learning it.

J. J. STEINFELD

A LIFE OF BOOKS

Shaun's books were scattered about his apartment. He began to gather them, piling one after another against a wall in even stacks. Then he began to count, at first each book individually, then by twos and threes: 587. Books shipped from city to city. Possessions he once couldn't bear to leave behind. Books even from elementary-school and junior-high-school days, and a copy of *The Little Engine That Could* from before he went to school, and every one of them read. But he no longer read, only looked at the books, helplessly attempting to recapture what they held and represented for him. The last books he had read were months ago, about theology: Thomas Merton and Karl Barth and Martin Buber. . . . Books from a night course on theology he had taken, attempting to ease back into university life after having dropped out nearly ten years ago. He had read the theology books with a desperate yearning, hoping that they would give him something to believe in, but he was unable to firm his hands onto any ledge of belief.

XXXX

Shaun's father walked into the living room. His face was flushed, and he was hitting his right hip hard with his right fist, so that even the four-year-old boy, pushing a little toy truck across the floor, knew the man was angry. Nerves, your father's nerves, was his mother's usual after-the-fact explanation to her son.

"Did you deface this book?" the man asked his son, holding the picture book open, his fist now outstretched fingers. Perched atop the train engine were small birds similar to those the four-year-old had seen on a tree outside his third-floor bedroom window. Some of the birds had toothy grins, others gloomy frowns, all the expressions human.

Shaun's mother hurried to the boy's side. "He doesn't know what *deface* means," she said to the man, cradling the child as if some debris were about to fall on his small body. The father was a large man, but capable of swift movement, and he bent down to the little boy. My daddy's bigger than the giant in *Jack and the Beanstalk*, way bigger, Shaun used to tell his playmates. *Jack and the Beanstalk* was the first book he recalled being read, by his father, the large man changing voices to fit the characters, performances filled with an awkward embrace of fatherhood, a love for his son temporarily soothing the indefinable discomfort he felt. Had Shaun heard his father's footsteps, he could have hidden himself in his room, with his other books and toys. He had a picture book about secret hiding places: forest, mountaintop, rooftop, deep under the ground. . . . The man held a page in front of his son's face, and demanded to know: "You draw these pictures?"

"He was only being a child," the mother defended her son.

"This is defacement. Books are not to be defaced." The man's hip-hitting resumed, becoming harder.

"Shaun loves that book. He knows every word of it."

The man grabbed the toy truck from the boy's hands. "This the little truck that could? This a pal of the little engine whose book you defaced?"

The little boy began to cry.

"He's taking after you already . . . whimpering," the man said, and went to the window. "The boy has to learn," he said, and threw the toy truck out the window, onto the small front lawn between their old apartment building and the sidewalk. "This book is no good anymore. It's defaced," he said, and threw the book out the window also. Then he began to apologize, to slap at his forehead in confusion and remorse. Later the mother went outside and found the toy truck and the book. A wheel had been broken off the toy and the book's cover was dirtied by damp soil and the grass that had been cut earlier in the day.

⋇⋇⋇

Shaun grabbed two armfuls of books, a few dropping as he opened the door, and made his way out of the building. One of the books he dropped, an anthology of travel writing, had been a birthday gift from his wife—*For My Dearest Booklover, Happy Reading and Happy 28th*, the inscription read— before they had separated two years ago. Maybe she'll send me a book when the divorce comes through, he thought, diluting his gloominess. He could remember the first time the topic had entered their conversation. "My parents are divorced . . . " Melanie had been smiling and laughing, and all of a sudden she made that disclosure, and Shaun remembered how coldly she had related that to him. "My mother is going to remarry," he had told her, managing to hold onto a smile. "I haven't met the guy yet. She wants me to be at the wedding. He's the subject of a chapter in a book on entrepreneurial success stories. People who have gone bankrupt and risen from the economic ashes. Not the stuff of mythology, if you ask me. My mother sent me two copies of the book. In one of the books, on the Table of Contents page, she wrote, 'I lucked out this time' . . . " That first evening, Melanie had said the expression *broken home*, we're both from broken homes, and Shaun had echoed it, and they both commented on how strange a choice of words it was—*broken home*. Broken apartment, Shaun had said, we lived in an apartment, a broken apartment. My father still lives in the same apartment, can you believe that? I stay with him when I'm going to school. Broken townhouse, we lived in a townhouse, a broken townhouse, Melanie said, and they were both laughing again. He had been thinking a great deal lately about their first time together, as if watching a play he had missed something in earlier and was determined to find the essential clues. When he reached the street he placed his books on the sidewalk.

✖✖✖

Shaun was waiting in the long checkout line, standing behind his shopping cart, and reading a book. A Margaret Laurence novel. He had searched for this edition of the book all over town, and had purchased it before coming to the grocery store.

He leaned against his shopping cart and it rolled into the woman in front of him. "I'm sorry," he said, pulling his cart away from the woman, and dropping the book. The hardback book, its covers flapping like a bird pushed off a branch, hit the woman on the foot.

"I didn't know a grocery store could be such a dangerous place," she said.

After apologizing several more times, and the woman assuring him she would live, though her entire life had raced past her eyes, Shaun, picking up the book, said, "I was arrested because of this book, when I was eighteen."

"You clobber an innocent soul with the book?" she said.

"A much sadder tale of misfortune," he told her, and smiled. "It would make a wonderful animated short."

"Not a major film? Surely your misfortune merits a full-length, big-budget feature."

When she saw the cover of the Laurence novel, she said she had read *The Stone Angel*, and enjoyed it greatly, but had never been arrested for anything. "You didn't really get arrested because of *The Stone Angel?*" she said, not yet able to get a handle on Shaun's sense of humor, a sense of humor she would love, even after she no longer loved him.

They had their first date not long after that, and spent the evening drinking beer and discussing books. "I've spent most of my two-year stay at university in the library, hiding—reading books that weren't assigned . . . looking for something, but not knowing what I was looking for . . . "

He told her he didn't know if he could finish the semester, had begun thinking of quitting. He had a job lined up in an electronics store. He pinched his left ear, and said, "Maybe I'll sell electronic devices until I hear my calling . . . " She had been considering taking a year off to travel. Europe. A literary excursion. I have compiled a list of writers' addresses, where they wrote or died . . . or did both. She took the list out of her backpack. You really do have a list, Shaun said. You think I'd lie to someone who'd dropped a Margaret Laurence hardback on my foot? The address of Sylvia Plath's final London residence was at the top of the list. I'll travel with you, he offered. I wouldn't mind seeing where some famous European philosophers did their philosophizing. Or maybe, where Somerset Maugham wrote *Of Human Bondage*. She accepted impulsively, and he said they just might wind up being inseparable. Then they told each other their names. "You think there's a novel somewhere with two characters named Melanie and Shaun?" she had asked. "It wouldn't take one of those infinite number of typing monkeys long to hit the keys for 'Shaun is smitten by Melanie,'" he said, and she said, "I'd rather have an infinite number of tiny, erudite mice at their keyboards . . . "

The first book he bought her was a pre-World War II travel guide to literary London, autographed by the author, and annotated throughout by the previous owner of the book. One of the annotations, which Melanie particularly liked, was "Met Beatrice in a restaurant not far from where H. G. Wells used to live as a young man . . . "

ЖОЖОЖ

As people walked by, Shaun offered them a book. Some refused, others accepted reluctantly, a few took the gifts with bewilderment and gratitude. A local prostitute who lived in the same building as Shaun blew him a kiss, told him she would be back for her book *after work*.

"I must have read this book about forty years ago. Bought it through a book club," the woman he had given *Of Human Bondage* to said. She skimmed through the book, glanced at sentences, read a sentence by the character Mildred in a lacklustre imitation of an English accent.

When Shaun had given away the first batch he returned to his room and brought down more books, this time carrying them in a large suitcase, which he opened on the sidewalk.

"Here, let me give you something for this. It's nearly new," a white-haired man said, reaching into his pocket.

"No, can't accept any money. I'm trying to bribe my way into bibliophile heaven," Shaun told him.

The man smiled and left, leafing through his book.

. . . Another refusal.

"But it's *Under the Volcano,*" Shaun said, with exaggerated emotion. "Malcolm Lowry wrote a lot of the book in British Columbia, but it's set in Mexico. The last video my wife and I saw together was *Under the Volcano,* so I have a sentimentality about the book and the film. I'm not absolutely sure, but I think she left me the same month we watched the film . . . "

This man quickened his pace and did not respond.

To another wary passer-by, the strange face covered with distrust, Shaun exclaimed, "Here, a sexy book. Female erotica, my friend." Still the man did not take the offering, or even stop. "Belonged to one of my aunts . . . "

To a woman Shaun gave away a Bible.

"You with a religious organization?" she inquired, sure he would ask her for money.

"Lord no . . . "

The woman smiled cautiously and walked away with her Bible.

"Read it as literature, and it's a sublime experience," Shaun called after her.

A stumbling man pleaded for a smoke, muttered a fragment of a grievous life story, and Shaun gave him a book by Northrop Frye. "I flunked the course," he told the man, "but it's a highly stimulating book . . ."

☒☒☒

Melanie moved hastily past the large man standing at the entrance to Shaun's room.

"In your own father's apartment," the man said, shaking his head at his son.

"I am in my room. You shouldn't come into my room."

"What a disregard of decency . . . "

Shaun stood up from the bed and went to the door, but his father blocked his exit.

"You holding me prisoner in my own room?"

"There has to be communication between us."

"I asked Melanie to marry me tonight. Actually, we asked each other to get married. Simultaneously."

"I guess I should wish you the best," Shaun's father said, his eyes glancing around the room, seeming to be searching for additional evidence of his son's wantonness, and saw a Bible on Shaun's desk. He walked over to the desk. "Is this the Bible your mother and I gave you for your high-school graduation?"

"You can check the inscription . . . "

"You put this Bible here to witness your engagement?"

"I'm working on a paper for school. There are other books on my desk."

Shaun's father picked up Northrop Frye's *The Great Code*: "You think I would enjoy this book?"

"Give it a try. Maybe you could help me with my paper."

"You sure you want to spend your life with Melanie?"

"I couldn't be surer of anything . . . "

ЖЖЖ

"This Sherlock Holmes collection was purchased in what had to be the tiniest bookstore in London. I bought it when I was overwhelmingly in love. On the same day we saw where Karl Marx wrote in the British Museum, where Sylvia Plath died, and where Charles Dickens pursued his immortality . . . "

A woman took the book and said she had been overwhelmingly in love once, but it lasted less than a day. He also handed out books he had purchased in France and Italy. "We did a literary trip, when my true love and I were in our early twenties," he explained.

Shaun continued on, one or two or three books to each person who would accept, until he tired and traded the street for his room. Later in the evening he returned to the street and completed the giveaway. Including the novel his mother had been reading when Shaun walked into the room and she told him she and his father would be separating.

"This book has inestimable sentimental value . . . "

Six or seven adults passed, before a young boy, about twelve, took the book. Shaun could see him arc the book into a trash container, a last-second shot to win the basketball game. Shaun yelled something about a nice shot, even if it was sacrilege. He thought of retrieving the book, but he didn't.

❊❊❊

"You know something," Shaun's mother said, a book open on her lap, tears flowing with her words, "I've never read *Of Human Bondage* before. I've seen the movie a bunch of times, three versions of the movie, in fact, but I've never read the book." He could stay a portion of the time with his father and the rest of the time with her. She attempted to steady her emotions: "You can keep half your books with your father here, and half with me. I found a new job I know I'm going to love. And best of all, I'm going to rent a little house. You'll have a backyard. You've lived all your life on the third floor of an apartment building . . . "

When Shaun turned away silently, she followed the moody fifteen-year-old to his room.

"Want to go to a bookstore? A new book for your collection."

Shaun looked at his neatly arranged collection, alphabetized by title. He began his counting at the first book on the first shelf, and tapped each book with his finger as he continued, saying the numbers aloud.

"We can spend the rest of the day visiting bookstores, Shaun . . . "

❊❊❊

"I do have something for your grandchildren," Shaun told the woman, and looked through the suitcase. Before he even found the book, he started to tell the story of *The Little Engine That Could,* and the woman joined with him in the refrain. He pulled the book out of the suitcase, and paused before handing it to the woman. "This book has the ability to fly . . . "

The woman saw *Das Kapital* in the suitcase, and asked if she could see it. "Better yet, it's yours," Shaun declared, a carnival barker's enthusiasm. "*Das Kapital* was from my Economic History course. Amazingly, I did quite well in that class . . . "

"We had a copy of this in our house when I was growing up. My parents were never Communists, but they liked discussing all ideologies."

"I had two copies of *Das Kapital,* one I purchased in a tiny bookstore in

London. I'd never seen such a tiny bookstore. Earlier in the day I'd visited
the British Museum, saw where Marx had worked. The proprietor of the
bookstore, a most English chap, told me that his grandfather had been
beaten up by his own father for joining the Communist Party. My father,
a staunchly apolitical man, never beat me, never even spanked me, but he
was prone to heave things out the window. He died a few months ago. I
went to visit him when he was dying. I didn't know how to comfort him.
I asked some stupid philosophical question about meaning or purpose. He
turned his head away—I thought to keep me from seeing him cry. I really
didn't know how to comfort my dying father. He started to tell the story of
The Little Engine That Could. Word for word. His voice was all rough, and
you could feel the agony. I thought he was going to die in the middle of the
story. I asked him if he remembered throwing my toy truck and book out
the window. He didn't remember that. Before he died, he told me he had
wanted to be an actor—had struggled for years. He gave up after I was born.
I never knew that. I grew up knowing that my mother was dissatisfied,
hated the jobs she did, wasn't the happiest wife the world has ever known.
But I always regarded my father as philosophical about the hand life had
dealt him. To me, my father always worked in construction. That's what
affected his nerves, my mother used to tell me. The noise. He hated the
noise, and he worked in construction. He died a week after my visit. He was
a marvelous reader. His performance of *Jack and the Beanstalk* occupies my
memory stage . . . "

XXXX

Shaun signed for the two large boxes, and the delivery man grumbled
that he had a lot of heavy boxes today. Shaun carried the first box into the
living room, then returned to the entranceway for the second one, and stood
holding it, performing some silent test of endurance. His mother came into
the room.

"My sister knew you love books, Shaun."

"I never thought of her as a reader. Except tabloids maybe."

"She had potential. Changed. When she was younger, she wanted to be
a writer."

"Aunt Phyllis?"

"She used to write me long letters that included the names of books she
recommended I read. With these wonderful little summaries."

Shaun carried the two boxes, one at a time, up to his room. Masking tape was crisscrossed over the boxes, and printed on a strip of masking tape of the first box was BOX 1 OF 2—POETRY AND FICTION, and on the second, BOX 2 OF 2—NON-FICTION. The first book he removed, from BOX 2 OF 2, a history of arctic exploration, contained an old love letter written to Phyllis, from another woman.

✕O✕O✕

The second to last book he gave away was to an off-duty police officer, who began to question Shaun. He explained what he had done, beginning to name some of the 587 titles, and the off-duty police officer said he was writing a gritty play in his spare time about the crime-and-drug scene in the area, and Shaun said he used to have a few theater-related books, but they had been given away, however he handed the off-duty police officer his *Bulfinch's Mythology*, telling the man it would be of great help in any writing. He also told him that his father had wanted to be an actor, and if life had been different, perhaps his father could have acted in the gritty play, and the off-duty police officer left satisfied that Shaun was not a threat to anyone.

✕O✕O✕

The three high-school friends had already finished a twelve pack of beer. It was the oldest one's nineteenth birthday. In the bookstore they were laughing and joking and daring each other to buy the sexiest book. That's one beautiful *Kama Sutra*. Love those illustrations. One of them dared the others to steal the sexiest book. They left the bookstore and walked around the downtown, discussing and commenting on the city life around them. When they reached another bookstore, a second-hand bookstore that had a window display of art books, blocks away, the plan was the first one to steal three books and make it to the hamburger joint down the street would be the winner, and the other two would treat him to supper, all he could eat.

"I was the only one to take a Canadian book," Shaun told the police officer who had arrested him and driven him to the police station.

"That make you special?"

"They're good books."

"Drinking, petty thievery, not a good way to go about your life."

"Nothing petty about *The Stone Angel*."

"Stealing is stealing, and unless you smarten up, you'll have plenty of time to read in jail . . . "

"I went for a hardback, that was a serious error in judgement. None of the others went for hardbacks. They looked for the thinnest paperbacks around."

ЖЖЖ

"You still here, honey?" the prostitute said to Shaun.

"It's been a long, tough day. Full of memories."

"Tell me about long and tough," the prostitute said. "Where are all your books?"

Shaun offered the woman his last book, and she took it. She read the title about theology, and said, "This ought to help me fall asleep tonight."

"You believe in God?" Shaun asked.

"Oh my, now that is the question of all questions. You should have asked me before I went off to work."

"So, what's your answer of all answers?"

"I believe in God, I most certainly do. I just wish God would have found me another line of work . . . "

The woman left, and Shaun stood there alone. He looked up at a streetlight, staring as if into another person's eyes. A little while later, a man with crutches stopped for a rest next to him, and Shaun lowered his eyes and said, "Both my father and the giant in *Jack and the Beanstalk* were as tall as that streetlight, and I'm not exaggerating. My mother, who had been dissatisfied with her lot in life, is embarking on a new life. I can't imagine getting married again." Shaun reached into his empty suitcase, wanting to give the departing stranger a book. "Had you been by earlier, I would have bestowed books like jewels on you," he called after the man.

Fighting away tears, Shaun walked towards a nearby bookstore, wondering what book he would buy to start his collection anew.

RICHARD KING PERKINS II

OF POETRY

Nearly every thought I have is of poetry. Not the words
or even the sounds of those words but the way stains
and color fade from the pavement month after year
until they live more inside me than on the gray roadway.
How they quietly transcribe me into their own ideas,
so subtly that I feel no different than the man I have
forgotten. That is the way it is with poetry. It redefines
constantly, always a little bit for the better. There are
very few things you can say that about. And those thoughts
that are not poetry: They have no place inside me, nor
in an old trunk kept in the slant beneath the stairs nor in
the dented gutter that slopes awkwardly away from my
writing window. I've never found a single one of them.
I've begun to suspect they may never have existed at all.

ANNA STEEGMANN

HERR GENAZINO AND I

"Choose a text to translate that will make you a better writer," Prof. Unger advised us.

Translating Wilhelm Genazino, one of Germany's most renowned writers, the author of twenty-nine books of which I had read twenty-seven, without a doubt would make me a better writer. I felt a special kinship to his melancholic characters, always on the brink of failure. His books prepared me for the hardships of the writer's life. Wilhelm Genazino struggled to find recognition as a writer. Financial success eluded him for more than two decades. But since 1990, he had won every major literary award in the German-speaking world. His works had been translated into Greek, Slovenian, Latvian, Russian, French, Italian, and Lithuanian.

My dream of becoming a writer lay torpid in prolonged hibernation until I revived it to study Creative Writing. In 2006, in my last semester at City College, I signed up for translation class. I knew that literature in translation counted for less than 0.5% of the US market; still I made it my mission to introduce Wilhelm Genazino to the American public. I had never translated a literary text. My sole publishing credits were a poem written twenty-five years ago and two academic texts. No one would let me translate a book. Maybe I could translate an essay from Genazino's collection *Der gedehnte Blick?*[i]

I emailed his publisher. A week later the director of foreign rights gave me permission to translate his essays. Then I panicked at my audacity of wanting to translate a writer who had been compared to Kafka. I read Walter Benjamin's *The Task of the Translator*, cleaned off my desk and placed my thirty-year-old *Langenscheidt's New College German Dictionary* next to my PC. I started with my favorite Genazino essay and typed the title. "A Gift That Fails. On the Lack of Literary Success." The first lines were easy. Then I hit a roadblock. *Kind* (child) was neuter in German, but could I translate the sentence as "it was bored?" Should I make the child male or female? Could I decide on the child's sex without knowing the author's intentions?

I wrote the director of foreign rights saying that I needed to consult with the author. She answered promptly. "Herr Genazino doesn't have a fax or an email account, but you may write to him." I tried to picture Beethovenstraße in Frankfurt. Was it a sad, tired neighborhood so often described in his books, the place where underemployed *flaneurs* stroll to escape the insanity of everyday life? Or did Herr Genazino live in quiet affluent Westend? After winning Germany's highest literary honor, the Georg-Büchner-Preis with its 40,000 Euro award, he should be able to afford a grand art nouveau apartment.

I wrote him how much I loved his books, how much they taught me about life. I told him that, after a long hiatus, I was giving writing another try and that I wrote in English now. Ten days later I received a reply. I stared at the envelope for a long time, the Luftpost sticker, the German castles on the stamps, the font type, and his address. One of Germany's most renowned writers had written to me, a literary nobody. Herr Genazino was delighted by my letter; delighted that I wanted to translate his essays. I could make the child a boy. Most important, Herr Genazino wished me success.

> . . . *I like that you didn't give up on writing. Do you know Beckett's wonderful line about not being able to go on, not being able to stop? I have been plowing through my Beckett collection for more than an hour now, but I cannot find the quote, at least not at this moment. Again, the ordinary demons of everyday life defeat the smallest moments of happiness.*
> *P.S. Please note that my name is Genazino, not Genanzino.*

I died 10,000 deaths and berated myself for having made such an unforgivable mistake. In my canon of Western Literature, next to Thomas Bernhard, Samuel Beckett was the greatest writer of the last century. Did Genazino refer to Fail. Fail again. Fail better? I had taped that quote to my bookshelf three years ago when I started to study creative writing.

The more I read Genazino, the more I fell in love with his writing. I brought his letter to translation class. My classmates were in awe. A real letter from a famous writer, a typewritten letter. I caught the translation bug. Professor Unger had warned us that it might happen. I never worked so hard on any text as I did translating his essays. I had to ponder every word. Genazino makes up words not found in any dictionary. He uses obsolete words from Bach motets and the writings of Martin Luther. Back then

Liebesblödigkeit meant love's frailty, weakness of the flesh. If I substituted it with the modern *Liebesblödheit* would it be love's bashfulness, imbecility, oafishness, or silliness?

Thinking of Herr Genazino, who waited more than twenty years for literary success, I was no longer afraid of literary failure, slush piles and competing with thousands of other aspiring writers. His letter was all the encouragement I needed. I submitted "A Gift That Fails" to Ingo Stoer, editor at *Dimension 2*. Two weeks later he accepted my translation for publication. I sent out a chapter of my memoir to a new literary journal. It was accepted. Well aware that a beginner should never submit her work to *The New York Times*, I sent an essay to *The New York Times*. "This might work for us," the editor responded.

I begged my friend Barbara Epler, editor-in-chief at New Directions to publish one of Genazino's novels. She chose *Ein Regenschirm für diesen Tag* and hired Philip Boehm as a translator. I was glad. Boehm had done a marvelous job with Kafka's *Letters to Milena*.

Wilhelm Genazino needed to know about my good luck. I sent him the essays I had translated. I told him I was going to be published in *The New York Times*. In his next letter he thanked me for sparking New Directions' interest in *Ein Regenschirm für diesen Tag* (An umbrella for this day). But he hated the American title *The Shoe Tester of Frankfurt*, in German, *ein Allerweltstitel*, an unremarkable, garden-variety title.

> *I cannot judge your translations. My English is not sufficient . . . . I trust the sound of your language, the cadences in your voice, your choice of complicated words. I admire that you were able to place an essay in the New York Times. I assume, it's difficult to get your foot in the door. I just finished a new novel . . . . As usual when I conclude a larger body of work, I feel as if there's nothing left to write, a sort of catastrophic scenario you might be familiar with too.*

I was surprised that a writer of his caliber and talent experienced such anguish. Writing, I felt fortunate, at ease, as if everything was possible. A year ago I had left my work as a school counselor to have more time to write. None of this might have happened if I had not written a letter to Wilhelm Genazino.

SNOWY GEMÜTLICHKEIT

The second snowstorm of this winter has arrived. A priceless stillness has fallen over New York. The city that never sleeps usually moves to a fast-paced soundtrack of honking horns, wailing sirens, and rumbling subways. Music blasts from windows and stores; vendors shout to attract customers. Street preachers pontificate to their impromptu flocks. People talk and argue louder and faster than any place I've ever visited.

Not this day. Not outside my window. St. Nicholas Avenue and St. Nicholas Park are blanketed with snow; the parked cars are buried under mountains of it. No one walks, no one shouts in the street. Except for the occasional sanitation department snowplow, the street is sparsely trafficked. The pristine white, the serenity, the brilliance of the winter sun, the unique winter light are a miracle to me—-not the weather emergency it is for the rest of the city. I can sit at my desk and devote a full day to my novel, look up and out once in a while to take in the serene city.

"So *gemütlich*," I think.

There is no word in the English language that accurately captures the meaning of *Gemüt* (mind, soul, disposition, heart) or *gemütlich* (comfortable, smug, and cozy). The term originally meant soulful (*voller Gemüt*). In the beginning of the 18th century *Gemütlichkeit* appeared in the writings of the Moravians in the sense of *Herzlichkeit* (cordiality, heartiness, warmth). In the Biedermeier period, *Gemütlichkeit* gained the new meaning of comfort or comfortableness and became a fashionable concept. At times *Gemütlichkeit* appeared related to nationalism and Teutonic mania and took on the negative connotation of laziness. The writer F. T. Vischer coined the derogatory untranslatable term *Vettermichelsgemütlichkeit* (cousin kraut's coziness?).

A word does not only carry linguistic and etymological meaning, it carries cultural as well as emotional meaning. In contrast to the common and valued emotional restraint, *Gemütlichkeit* is an acceptable way of expressing emotions in German culture. It's a way of making oneself and others feel at home, to let down one's guard and experience intimacy. My own etymology, origin and meaning of the word *Gemütlichkeit* stems from the Germany of the 60s. I was invited for *Kaffee und Kuchen* (coffee and cake) by my neighbor, Frau Stanke. Sitting across from her on the kitchen bench, I watched her set the table with ritualistic accuracy and care for her ten-year-old visitor with the linen tablecloth (picked up earlier in the day from the Heissmangel pressing service), the gold trimmed Sunday china, a platter of poppy seed cake, a cup of Muckefuck (ersatz coffee) for me and the cup of Jacobs Krönung for herself. She squeezed her massive body into the narrow space on the bench and slid closer to me. Then came the precious invitation in her charming Silesian accent:

Lass es uns gemütlich machen. Let's get comfortable.

A LOSS BEYOND WORDS

In the air, on my way from Berlin to New York I finish Monika Maron's *Ach Glueck* somewhere above Newfoundland. The sparse and forlorn prose, the author's questions about happiness in old age and the role of fate in our lives, speak to me. Like the protagonist, I am on a transatlantic flight headed into a new scary life, a future much different from how I envisioned it months ago. Maron's protagonist is leaving behind her husband in Berlin. My husband died and left me behind.

I take out my notebook to add to my bloated to-do list. English words appear on the paper. I am surprised. After more than five weeks reading, speaking and writing German, my brain has switched over to English. I wasn't aware of it. I take it as a good sign.

On April 4 I brought Roman to the emergency room of Mount Sinai Hospital. Language was my refuge for the twenty-three terrifying days that followed. I woke up after a few hours of restless sleep and sat down at my computer. I wrote friends asking for help and prayers. I gave updates following his twelve-and-a-half hours of brain surgery. I told them about the diagnosis of Schwannoma and my relief at finding out that it was a benign tumor. I wrote about the complications and setbacks, his optimism and his plans for the future. He was looking forward to Christmas in Goerlitz, Easter in Vienna, and summer in Venice. He promised to take me for a ride on the Siberian Railroad once he retired.

On Wednesday, April 27 I wrote the final message: *Roman died this afternoon.*

X X X

I wrote the obituary for his memorial service for I could not bear the idea of a stranger delivering the final words of farewell. Then the English language failed me. I was struck speechless. I could barely write. When I scribbled down a few paragraphs into my journal, it was in German. I have resided in a place without written language ever since.

Living in a new land, the land of the grieving, I live with tears, pain, despair, but also gratitude and love. I cannot shape these emotions into words, sentences and paragraphs. They are too raw and too unruly for words. Roman was my husband, my best friend, my life companion for twenty-five years. A loss beyond words.

It has been four months since Roman left this world. He lives in my heart, in the cells of my body, and in my memories. He lives on in the hearts and memories of his friends, his family, his students and colleagues. He visits me in my dreams, takes me in his arms and comforts me.

The English language is the second language for both of us. We spoke to each other in English, we argued with each other and expressed our love for each other in English. A language made precious because he told me several times each day that he loved me.

I hope to make him proud by going on living and writing.

JOHN SIBLEY WILLIAMS

TERMINUS

It makes no difference if the future is ash spread across the sea
or if granite speaks for our impermanence.
It makes no difference that snow is a language,
my body is time, that reading is *reading into*,
both unity and divergence are illusions.

With the first real thing placed in my hands came "what?,"
and other questions until I was no longer a child.

It makes no difference if the answers are born
of imagination or dust.
However it ends, the moment before I'll still be
a curious specimen homed in a body at least I tried to explain.

MEMORY

Like a house,
it depends on structure.
Walls to withstand weather and dust.
A window to release the unbreathable air.

There must be floorboards beneath.
Photographs to keep us from falling
too far from the past.
And within the frame
that limits our bodies
glass
and an image grown distant.

The how of remembering
runs the full length of the mirror
and is contained, and changed.
To touch the surface
behind our surface
is an act of self-translucence.

Memory is a decision,
like loving,
like where to drive the nails
into everything we've loved
intensely, for a time.

WE ARE ALL ICE FISHERMEN

Through the hole an axe fractures from ice
we see things are not as frozen as they appear.
Darting gills. Silver flashes of life beneath
a winter surface. An entire, knowable city yawns,
feeds and in turn is devoured.

That is how it is here. I've read
that is how it's always been.
Yet we forget with each penetrating chill.
We assume the world mirrors,
must be lifeless and frozen to core.

Because we've buried
everything we once loved.
Because azaleas haven't flowered
over an earth we haven't tilled.
Just because the hard-packed snow
our children build men from
melts unnoticed, leaving
the absence of a figure—

each time we must go to the lake
alone and relearn
the guilt from surviving our friends
can be unworn, like a parka
when the sky has thawed.

ACKNOWLEDGEMENTS

Debra Bacharach's "Fire, Aphasia, and the Spirit World" first appeared in *Literary Mama*.

Barbara Crooker previously published "Le Temps Perdu" in *Bhatan Today* and "Weather Report" in *Calyx*.

"Half Baked" by Hannah Tolman Flannery previously appeared in *Mother as Writer: A Delicate Balance*, ed. Elizabeth Anderson (Xlibris) and in *Not a Muse: The Inner Lives of Women*, ed. Kate Rogers and Vicki Homes (Haven Books) while "The Unfinished Project" appeared in a different form in *After Hours*.

Paul Hostovsky's "Merton" is from his collection *Naming Names* (Main Street Rag) while "The Cat Is Sleeping on a Draft of This Poem" was previously published in *IthacaLit*.

Katharyn Howd Machan previously published "Washing the Rich Man's Porch" in *The Kerf* and "With All My People Dead" in *Nimrod* while "How Not to Write a Poem" is from her collection *H* (Gribble Press).

"Atelier" is from Mike Maggio's collection *Sifting through the Madness* (Xlibris).

"The Ailing Poem" by John Manesis appears in his collection *With All My Breath* (Cosmos).

Michael Onofrey's "Klimt" previously appeared in *Willard & Maple*.

Both "A Life of Books" and "Past Artistry" by J.J. Steinfeld were published in his collection *Disturbing Identities* (Ekstasis).

Don Thackrey's "The Verse Roundup" was published in *Word Catalyst Magazine* and "Fence for Verse" in *Lucid Rhythms*.

Photographs by Heather Tosteson.

CONTRIBUTORS

Deborah Bacharach is a poet and essayist. Her work has appeared in *New Letters*, *The Antigonish Review*, *Cimmaron Review*, and *Blue Lyra Review* among many others. Her book of poetry, *After I Stop Lying*, is forthcoming from Wordtech Communications. She is a writing teacher and tutor in the Seattle area.

Patricia Barone's *The Scent of Water*, a collection of poetry, is out from Blue Light Press. *The Wind*, a novella, and *Handmade Paper*, poetry, were Minnesota Voices Award winners and published by New Rivers Press. Her short stories appeared in Wising Up Press, Peter Lang, and Plume/Penguin anthologies. She has received a Loft-McKnight Award of Distinction and a Lake Superior Contemporary Writers Award.

Barbara Crooker's poems have appeared in journals such as *The Hollins Critic*, *The Beloit Poetry Journal*, *America*, and *The Green Mountains Review*, and anthologies including *The Bedford Introduction to Literature* and *Good Poems American Places*. Her newest book is *Gold* (Cascade Books, 2013), and her poetry has been read many times on *The Writer's Almanac*.

Vida Cross received MFAs in both writing and filmmaking from Art Institute of Chicago and her MA in English from Iowa State. A Cave Canem Fellow (2007-2013), she received honorable mention for her book manuscript *Bronzeville at Night: 1945* in Cave Canem's 2010 First Book Poetry Award. She has published in *Tabula Poetica*, *Transitions*, *Cave Canem Anthology XII: Poems 2008-2009*, *The Literary Review*, *Reed Magazine*, and *The Journal of Film and Video*.

Deborah Pratt Curtiss has devoted fifty-plus years of her life to painting/ exhibiting, forty to studying/performing music, thirty-five to studying dance, and twenty-five to (published) informational writing. Barely three years ago she began to explore creative non-fiction; "Going Nude" is her first creative essay to be published.

Maureen Tolman Flannery's volumes of poems include *Tunnel into Morning, Destiny Whispers to the Beloved, A Fine Line,* and *Ancestors in the Landscape.* She is also a wood-carver, toy-maker, and home funeral guide. Her poems have appeared in a hundred anthologies and two hundred literary journals, including *Atlanta Review, Santa Fe Literary Review, Poetry East,* and *Birmingham Poetry Review.*

Diane Giardi, MFA, is an artist, arts educator and poet. Her work has been published, among others, in *The Yale Journal of Humanities in Medicine, Long Island Sounds, The Endicott Review, The Wilderness House Literary Review, Ann Arbor Review, Muddy River Poetry Review, Moon Magazine, Kind of a Hurricane Press, The Path Magazine, Chuffed Buff Books, Minerva Rising* and *Dovetail Publishing.*

Jo Going's poetry is rooted in the iconography of the Alaska wilderness. She is also a visual artist, and all of her poems have a related work of art. Books of her art and poetry are in museum collections in the Museum of Modern Art in New York and the National Museum of Women in the Arts in Washington, DC.

Jim Govoni is a psychotherapist with degrees in business, art education and counseling. Jim's long standing interest in art, yoga and Jungian psychology led him into poetry as a way to bring meaning into the second half of life. This anthology contains his first published poem.

John Grey is an Australian-born poet and US resident since the late seventies who works as a financial systems analyst. He has recently published in *Nerve Cowboy, Freshwater* and *Over The Transom* with work upcoming in *Abbey, Advocate, Alchemy* and *Aurorean.*

Patrick Hansel has published poems in twenty journals, including *Hawai'i Pacific Review, Painted Bride Quarterly, Passager, Perfume River Poetry Review,* and *The Meadowland Review.* He was selected for the 2008-09 Mentor Series at the Loft Literary Center in Minnesota, and was a 2011 Minnesota State Arts Board Artist Initiative grantee. His novella *Searching* was serialized in thirty-three issues of *The Alley News.*

Michael Hess is a filmmaker and writer who lives in Toronto. His films have played at the NYU Directors Series, NewFest, the American Cinemateque in Los Angeles, the Kansas International Film Festival and the Beloit International Film Festival. His writing has appeared in *Shenandoah, Glassworks, Red Savina Review, The Outrider Review, AlleyCat News* and *Glitterwolf Magazine.*

Paul Hostovsky is the author of six books of poetry, including most recently *Selected Poems* (2014, FutureCycle Press). His poems have won a Pushcart Prize and two Best of the Net Awards. He has been featured on Poetry Daily, Verse Daily, and The Writer's Almanac. He was a Featured Poet on the Georgia Poetry Circuit 2013. He makes his living in Boston as an interpreter for the deaf.

Céline Keating is a writer, editor, and music reviewer. *Play for Me,* her second novel, will be published in May 2015. Her short fiction has been published in many literary magazines, including *Echoes, North Stone Review, Santa Clara Review,* and *Prairie Schooner.* Her nonfiction has appeared in *Acoustic Guitar,* minor7th.com, *Coastal Living,* and *Poets & Writers.* She lives in New York, N.Y.

Tom Leskiw and his wife Sue and their dog Zevon live near Eureka, California. He retired in 2009 following a thirty-one-year career as a hydrologic/biologic technician for Six Rivers National Forest. His research, essays, book and movie reviews have appeared in a variety of scientific and literary journals.

Katharyn Howd Machan is the author of thirty-two published collections, and her poems have appeared in numerous magazines, anthologies, and textbooks, including *The Bedford Introduction to Literature* and *Sound and Sense.* She is a full professor in the Department of Writing at Ithaca College in central New York State. In 2012 she edited *Adrienne Rich: A Tribute Anthology* (Split Oak Press).

Mike Maggio has published fiction, poetry, travel and reviews in *Potomac Review, The Montserrat Review, Pleiades, Apalachee Quarterly, The Northern Virginia Review, The L.A. Weekly.* His books are: *Oranges From Palestine* (Mardi Gras Press, 1996), *Sifting Through the Madness* (Xlibris, 2001), *deMOCKcracy* (Plain View Press, 2007), The Keepers (March Street Press, 2011), and *The Wizard and the White House* (Little Feather Press, 2014).

John Manesis, a retired physician, has published his poetry in ninety literary publications, including *Wisconsin Review, North Dakota Quarterly and Hospital Drive*. Five of his poetry books have been published, the most recent being, *In the Third Season*.

Milton Montague, after seventeen years as a senior auditor at Hunter College, was turned on by poetry courses and began recording his memories of a long life from The Great Depression, World War II, love, marriage, children, business with the rich and famous, and retirement. His poems have appeared in, among others, *Poetica, Dirty Chai, and On the Rusk*. Turning ninety, he is delighted with this new stage in his life.

Michael Onofrey, in addition to having been published in *Illness & Grace, Terror & Transformation* (Wising Up Press), has had his short stories published in *Cottonwood, The Evansville Review, Natural Bridge, Road to Nowhere and Other New Stories from the Southwest* (University of New Mexico Press), and *Weber—The Contemporary West*.

Carl "Papa" Palmer, retired Army, retired FAA, now just plain retired, lives in University Place, WA. He has seven chapbooks and a contest-winning poem riding buses somewhere in Seattle. Carl has been nominated for the Micro Award and Pushcart Prize. Motto: Long Weekends Forever.

Richard King Perkins II is a state-sponsored advocate for residents in long-term care facilities. A three-time Pushcart nominee and a Best of the Net nominee, his work has appeared in hundreds of publications including *Poetry Salzburg Review, Bluestem, Emrys Journal, Sierra Nevada Review, Two Thirds North, The Red Cedar Review* and *December Magazine* and forthcoming in *Broad River Review, The William and Mary Review* and *The Louisiana Review*.

Mary Kay Rummel is the first Poet Laureate of Ventura County, California. Her seventh book of poetry, *The Lifeline Trembles*, is winner of the 2014 Blue Light Poetry Prize. Previously, *What's Left Is The Singing* was also published by Blue Light Press of San Francisco. She teaches at California State University, Channel Islands and divides her time between Minneapolis and Ventura.

Frank Salvidio, a retired English professor whose poetry has appeared in journals and anthologies, is the author of *Between Troy & Florence* (original poems and translations) and *Inventing Love: A Sonnet Sequence*, as well as translations of Dante (*Inferno, Vita Nuova*) and Sappho of Lesbos (*Sappho Says*).

Ira Schaeffer lives in Warwick and teaches English at the Community College of Rhode Island. In conjunction with Stone & Plank, Inverse, and Ocean State Poets, Ira has offered poetry readings at numerous venues throughout Rhode Island. His recent poetry has appeared *Penumbra, On the Dark Side: An Anthology of Fairy Tale Poetry, and 50 Haiku.*

Ruth Margolin Silin, mother of three, grandmother of seven and former director of development at a pediatric hospital, is now semi-retired with more wonderful time for poetry as well as helping out at her daughter's boutique. Her poems have appeared in *Main Street Rag, Ibbetson Street, Hazmat Review, Love After 70* (Wising Up Press), and other journals and anthologies.

Laurence Snydal is a poet, musician and retired teacher. He has published more than a hundred poems in such magazines as *Columbia, Caperock, Lyric* and *Gulf Stream* and in many anthologies including *The Year's Best Fantasy and Horror, The Pagan's Muse* and *Visiting Frost*. Some of his work has been performed in New York City and Baltimore.

Alan Swyer is an award-winning filmmaker, including documentaries on Eastern spirituality in the Western world, the criminal justice system, diabetes, and boxing. Other credits include "Rebound" and "The Buddy Holly Story." He produced an album of Ray Charles love songs and has worked with artists Solomon Burke, Billy Preston, and Ike Turner. His fiction has appeared in Ireland, England, and in several American publications.

Anna Steegmann, a native of Germany, lives in New York City. She has translated books and essays from German to English, published film scripts, radio features, journalistic texts, essays and short stories in both languages. She earns her living as a wandering adjunct at several CUNY colleges.

J. J. Steinfeld is a Canadian fiction writer, poet, and playwright living on Prince Edward Island. He has published fourteen books, including *Would You Hide Me?* (stories, Gaspereau Press), *An Affection for Precipices* (poetry, Serengeti Press), *Misshapenness* (poetry, Ekstasis Editions), and *A Glass Shard and Memory* (stories, Recliner Books). Over forty of his one-act plays and a handful of full-length plays have been performed in Canada and the United States.

Don Thackrey lives in Dexter, Michigan, where he is retired from teaching and administering at the University of Michigan. His prose publications include a book on Emily Dickinson and his verse has been published in online and printed journals and in anthologies. A book of his verse is forthcoming from the Dakota Institute Press.

Hannah Thomassen lives and writes in the forested foothills of Oregon's Cascade Mountains. Her work has appeared in *Big Bridge, Presence, Windfall, Verseweavers, Voice Catcher, Bird's Thumb* and two previous anthologies from Wising Up Press. In one life she was a teacher, and in another, an RN. All her lives have been rich and instructive.

Claudia Van Gerven has been published in numerous journals, including *Prairie Schooner, Louisiana Review, Calyx, Georgetown Review,* and *Lullwater Review,* as well as in numerous anthologies. Her chapbook, *The Ends of Sunbonnet Sue,* won the Angel Fish Press Prize and *Amazing Grace* was nominated for a Pushcart Prize. Her latest chapbook, *Bearing Witness,* is forthcoming from Finishing Line Press.

Bill Vernon served in the United States Marine Corps, studied English literature, then taught it. Writing is his therapy, along with exercising outdoors and doing international folkdances. Five Star Mysteries published his novel *Old Town* in 2005, and his poems, stories and nonfiction have appeared in a variety of magazines and anthologies.

Rosemary Volz has published short stories in *Blueline, Event, Nebo* and *Another Chicago Magazine.* Her poetry has appeared in *Evening Street Review, Reader's Choice, Earth's Daughter, Write Wing Publishing, Conversations Across Borders, Baseball Bard, Third Wednesday* and *Hospital Drive.* She recently won the Flagler County Poet's Award. She is now associated with the Tomoka Poets and lives in Ponce Inlet, Florida.

Joel Wachman is a writer and computer technologist. He has written for *Harvard Review* and *The Boston Globe*, and has won awards for his works of creative nonfiction. His self-published zine, *Par Avion*, was acclaimed by the ex-patriot community in Paris in the 1990s. "The Ownership of Desire" is based on a true story he overheard during that time.

Petra Dai Walech is a freelance writer and actor living in Los Angeles whose home in writing has always been poetry; her motivation lies in trying to make audible what her heart sees. When she is not auditioning or writing, she is likely lost in the mountains on a hike or running alongside the ocean.

John Sibley Williams is the author of eight collections, most recently *Controlled Hallucinations* (FutureCycle Press, 2013). John serves as editor of *The Inflectionist Review* and board member of the Friends of William Stafford. Previous publishing credits include: *American Literary Review, Third Coast, Nimrod, Rio Grande Review, Inkwell, Bryant Literary Review, RHINO,* and various anthologies. He lives in Portland, Oregon.

Tyree Deshawn Wilson is a twenty-six year-old Ohio resident. As of this writing, he works at a library full-time as a circulation clerk. He hopes to one day have a bio that is truly noteworthy.

GUEST EDITORS

Kerry Langan is the author of two collections of short fiction, *Only Beautiful & Other Stories* and *Live Your Life & Other Stories*. Her short stories have been published in dozens of literary magazines and anthologized often. Her non-fiction has appeared in *Working Mother* and *Shifting Balance Sheets: Women's Stories of Naturalized Citizenship and Cultural Attachment* (Wising Up Press). She is currently at work on her next collection of short stories. She resides with her family in Oberlin, Ohio.

Michele Markarian is a writer/actor whose plays have been produced across the US and the UK. Michele's short stories have appeared in four anthologies by Wising Up Press, *Mom's Literary Magazine*, *yesteryearfiction.com*, *The Journal of Microliterature*, and the anthology *inherplace.org*. Her plays have been published by Dramatic Publishing, Heuer Publishing, Oxford University Press, and Smith & Kraus. She can occasionally be seen reading from her high school journals as part of Mortified Boston. Michele is a member of the Dramatists Guild.

EDITORS/PUBLISHERS

HEATHER TOSTESON is the author of *Breathing in Portuguese, Living in English; Germs of Truth; The Sanctity of the Moment: Poems from Four Decades; Visible Signs;* and *God Speaks My Language, Can You?* She has worked as executive editor of two public health journals and in health communications with a focus on communication across disciplines, racism, social trust, and how belief systems develop and change. She holds an MFA in Creative Writing (UNC-Greensboro) and PhD in English and Creative Writing (Ohio University).

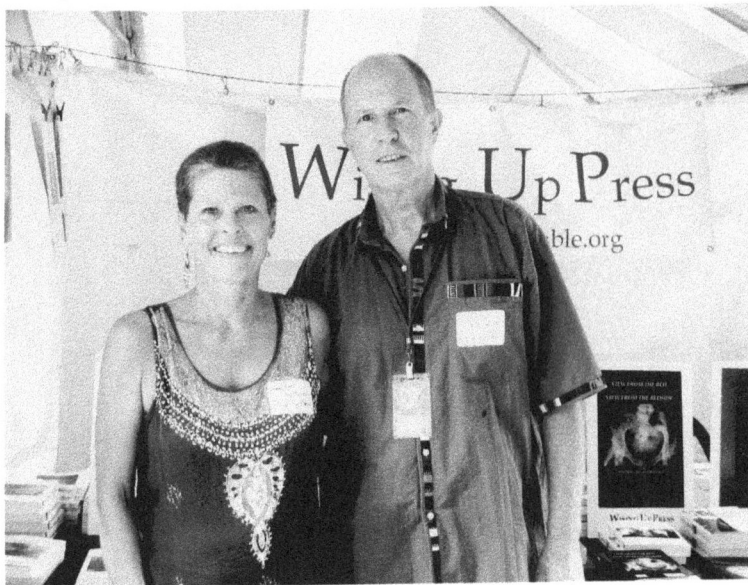

CHARLES BROCKETT has a PhD from UNC-Chapel Hill and is a recipient of several Fulbright and National Endowment for the Humanities awards. A retired political science professor, he has written two well-received books on Central America, *Land, Power, and Poverty* and *Political Movements and Violence,* and numerous social science journal articles and book chapters. With Heather Tosteson, he is co-founder of Universal Table and Wising Up Press and co-editor of the Wising Up Anthologies.

See our booklist and calls for submissions for new anthologies
www.universaltable.org
wisingup@universaltable.org

www.ingramcontent.com/pod-product-compliance
Lightning Source LLC
Chambersburg PA
CBHW020244290326
41930CB00038B/260